ALCOHOL, CRIME AND PUBLIC HEALTH

Alcohol, Crime and Public Health explores the issue of drinking in the criminal justice system, providing an overview of the topic from both a criminal justice and a public health perspective. The majority of prisoners in the UK (70%) have an alcohol use disorder, and evidence tells us that risky drinking is high amongst those in contact with all areas of the criminal justice system.

Uniquely, this book brings both a criminal justice and a public health perspective to the topic. The book opens by exploring the levels of crime attributed to alcohol, the policy context of alcohol and crime, and the prevalence of risky alcohol consumption in the criminal justice system. The following chapters examine risky drinking amongst men, women and young people in the criminal justice system. The final chapters look at the efficacy of psychosocial interventions for risky drinking in the criminal justice system, and look forward to how researchers and practitioners can work together to produce research in the criminal justice system.

Written in an accessible and concise style, *Alcohol, Crime and Public Health* will be of great use to students of criminology, criminal justice and public health as well as the wider area of public and social policy in relation to alcohol and crime.

Dorothy Newbury-Birch is Professor of Alcohol and Public Health Research at Teesside University, UK. She leads a team of researchers and students in work around co-producing public health research in various settings including the criminal justice system. Professor Newbury-Birch is a world-leading expert in work around reducing alcohol-related harm in society, particularly for young people and those in various stages of the criminal justice system.

Jennifer Ferguson is a lecturer in Criminology and a senior researcher in the School of Social Sciences, Humanities & Law at Teesside University, UK. Jennifer comes from a legal background, having completed her law degree and Legal Practice Course (LPC) in 2010. She has been working as a researcher since 2011 on various alcohol projects and has moved more towards research in the criminal justice system. Her research expertise includes alcohol-related harm in the criminal justice setting.

ROUTLEDGE STUDIES IN CRIME AND SOCIETY

ALCOHOL, CRIME AND PUBLIC HEALTH

Dorothy Newbury-Birch and Jennifer Ferguson

LONDON AND NEW YORK

Designed cover image: © gettyimages.com

First published 2023
by Routledge
4 Park Square, Milton Park, Abingdon, Oxon OX14 4RN

and by Routledge
605 Third Avenue, New York, NY 10158

Routledge is an imprint of the Taylor & Francis Group, an informa business

British Library Cataloguing-in-Publication Data
A catalogue record for this book is available from the British Library

Library of Congress Cataloging-in-Publication Data
Names: Newbury-Birch, Dorothy, author. |
Ferguson, Jennifer (Lecturer in criminology), author.
Title: Alcohol, crime and public health /
Dorothy Newbury-Birch and Jennifer Ferguson.
Description: Abingdon, Oxon ; New York, NY : Routledge, 2023. |
Series: Routledge studies in crime and society |
Includes bibliographical references and index.
Identifiers: LCCN 2022058587 (print) | LCCN 2022058588 (ebook) |
ISBN 9780367771058 (hardback) | ISBN 9780367771034 (paperback) |
ISBN 9781003169802 (ebook)
Subjects: LCSH: Prisoners–Alcohol use–Great Britain. |
Alcoholism–Great Britain. | Criminal justice, Administration–Great Britain. |
Criminal statistics–Great Britain. | Public health–Great Britain.
Classification: LCC HV8836.5 .N456 2023 (print) |
LCC HV8836.5 (ebook) | DDC 362.2920973–dc23/eng/20230302
LC record available at https://lccn.loc.gov/2022058587
LC ebook record available at https://lccn.loc.gov/2022058588

ISBN: 978-0-367-77105-8 (hbk)
ISBN: 978-0-367-77103-4 (pbk)
ISBN: 978-1-003-16980-2 (ebk)

DOI: 10.4324/9781003169802

Typeset in Bembo
by Newgen Publishing UK

For Sophia, Harry and Molly who make us smile every day.

CONTENTS

FIGURES

TABLES

ABBREVIATIONS

ABI	alcohol brief interventions
ASBI	alcohol screening and brief intervention
SBI	screening and brief intervention
AUD	alcohol use disorder
AUDIT	alcohol use disorders identification test
CJS	criminal justice system
HMPPS	Her Majesty's Prison and Probation Service
NHS	National Health Service
MOJ	Ministry of Justice
MI	motivational interviewing
ROTL	release on temporary licence

ACKNOWLEDGEMENTS

As academics, we were aware that it is really difficult to do research around health conditions in the criminal justice system. You must navigate funding which may require either crime or health as a primary outcome as well as the necessary ethical approvals in both a health and a criminal justice system which can take a long time. However, after 20 years of working in the field of testing alcohol interventions in various stages of the criminal justice system, which has included systematic reviews, evaluations and randomised controlled trials, we have realised the need for much more research in this area. Furthermore, we realised that a book was needed to explain the issues and help future researchers and academics working in the field.

We wrote this book as academics in the field; however, we also wrote it as mother and daughter. Jennifer followed Dorothy into the same academic field and has become a senior member of her team and Dorothy is very proud to have written this book with her.

It is always difficult to find the time to write a book, always seems a great idea before you start and then you must actually write it. We were hit by the COVID-19 pandemic as well, which meant that our way of working as academics changed, so we had to find time to write the 'actual' book. Jennifer was finishing her PhD and home schooling two children and Dorothy had to change a high number of research projects, but we did it and we are proud of it. We are so grateful to leave this as a living memory of the work we have done together and thank our husbands (Mark and James) and Jennifer's children Sophia and Harry as well as Jennifer's sister Stephanie, partner Jack and baby Molly. Sophia, Harry and Molly are the joys of our lives.

There are so many other people to thank. Thank you to Routledge for giving us the opportunity to write this book and being so understanding to our requests for extensions. Thank you Team Alpha who are the amazing group of people in the School of Social Sciences, Humanities and Law at Teesside University and who make up our research team for helping not only with the book but also taking other stuff of our plates so we could have 'the little bit of time' we had to write it. Thank you to the amazing Dr Gillian Waller, who began her career as a PhD student with Dorothy and wrote Chapter 2 for us. She is a great academic, researcher and friend. Thanks also to Dr Natalie Connor and Dr Andy Divers for taking work of our plates for us to write this. Thanks also to Emma Cuthbertson, who is our fabulous administrative assistant who ensures we are in the correct place at the correct time with the correct paperwork. 'Everyone needs an Emma'.

Dorothy would like to thank friends at Bhalo Pahar in West Bengal and Kaushik Chatterjee in Kolkata for giving her the space in November 2022 to complete the final chapter. Part of her heart will always belong there.

Finally, and importantly, thank you to all the researchers and academics who are moving the work forward in this area. To the practitioners and policymakers who work in the criminal justice system and who are looking to us, as academics and researchers, to develop evidence-based interventions, and to those people who are involved in the criminal justice system who have taken their time to take part in research. We really are very grateful.

We hope you enjoy the book.

GLOSSARY

Alcohol brief intervention: A short, evidence-based, structured conversation about alcohol consumption with a patient that seeks in a non-confrontational way to motivate and support the individual to think about and/or plan a change in their drinking behavior in order to reduce their consumption and/or their risk of harm.

Screening and brief interventions: Those practices that aim to identify a real of potential alcohol problem and motivate and individual to do something about it.

Alcohol use disorder: Someone who is drinking at a hazardous, harmful or dependent level, as identified by a screening tool.

Prison category: In the UK, there are different types of prison: closed prisons where prisoners cannot be trusted to leave and escape must be made difficult, and open prisons, which with permission, prisoners can leave temporarily. These are split into different categories: Category A, B, C and D for men but only open and closed for women.

Open prison: Residents are able to leave the prison temporarily, have keys to their own rooms and there are no large fences or walls for security.

Stages of prison: The different stages of prison are initial entry to prison; establishing routine in the prison; then either, liberation from prison, or being moved to a lower category prison.

Reception into prison: The process of being booked in to prison. All paperwork is filled in and searches are carried out.

Sentenced prisoner: Someone who is incarcerated and has received a sentence.

Remand prisoner: Someone who is incarcerated and waiting adjudication.

Release on temporary licence (ROTL): Being able to leave prison for a short period of time to help settle into the community before release/take part in paid or unpaid work.

Peer prisoner: A prisoner who has a job in the prison to carry out various roles, for example, induction into the prison.

Listener: A prisoner who is trained by the Samaritans to volunteer as a support mechanism for other prisoners.

1

WHAT DO WE MEAN BY PUBLIC HEALTH, CRIMINAL JUSTICE AND ALCOHOL USE DISORDERS?

Introduction

Alcohol consumption and the related harms continue to be a significant public health issue across the world (1, 2). The effects of alcohol not only impact on the health and well-being of individuals, but they can also be observed broadly across families, friends and the wider population. One of the associated harms of alcohol is the link between consumption and crime and antisocial behaviour. Recent data from the Crime Survey, for England and Wales, shows that in about half of all violent crimes, the victim perceived the offender to be under the influence of alcohol (3). Therefore, addressing alcohol consumption across a population remains to be a fundamental strategy when considering how to tackle crime. However, it has been shown that there is a complex interplay between individual and contextual factors and risky drinking behaviours and alcohol-related crime (4). This chapter will explore these issues.

An estimated 4% of worldwide deaths and 4–6% of global disability-adjusted life-years are linked to alcohol (5). Globally alcohol is the sixth most important risk factor for ill health and premature death (1, 2). There is evidence of an association between increased alcohol consumption and coronary heart disease, hypertension, haemorrhagic and ischaemic stroke, alcoholic liver disease and a range of cancers (6).

Reduction in alcohol consumption is essential to achieve global targets of reducing deaths from non-communicable diseases by 25% between 2010 and 2025 (7). Heavy drinkers who reduce their drinking reduce their risk of mortality in comparison to those who continue heavy drinking (8). The higher the level of drinking, the stronger the effects of a given reduction (1, 9).

Although the relationship is complex, there is an association between alcohol use and offending behaviour (10, 11), with an interplay between the amount

DOI: 10.4324/9781003169802-1

drank, the pattern of drinking, and individual and contextual factors (12). It has been shown that the frequent coexistence of alcohol and violence does not evidence a universal or causal link. Rather it points to a culturally contingent association between alcohol and violence with drinking being a contributory cause of violence alongside other factors, including individual characteristics and contextual factors (13–16). However, it must be remembered that the consumption of alcoholic drinks is an important feature of leisure in Western societies (17). Pleasure in drinking can be found simply not only in the enjoyment of taste, but also in the way it enhances personal relaxation, sociability and recreation (17). The understanding of alcohol is not fully understood and acutely ambivalent: drinking is widely enjoyed yet frequently linked to many social problems (18). We know that consciousness-changing substances used for pleasure are a constant target for legal action because they jeopardise either order on the streets or the health of those who enjoy them. Laws governing the sale, possession or consumption of such substances are tightened continuously but can be enforced only selectively, to avoid criminalising swathes of young people. A huge and permanent disjunction exists between the policies and prognostications of the criminal justice, politicians and the media, and the views and practices of young people as a whole. Drug-advice agencies find their expertise consistently undervalued (19–21).

Hazardous drinking is a repeated pattern of drinking that increases the risk of psychological or physical problems (22), whereas harmful drinking is defined by the presence of these problems (23). Drinking at hazardous or harmful levels is categorised as risky drinking. Previous research has shown that risky drinking is more than twice as high in the criminal justice system in comparison with the general population in the UK, and probable dependency up to ten times higher (24).

The alcohol industry

Measham and Brain argue that the pursuit of altered states of intoxication must be positioned in late modern society as a behaviour which is a vehicle for consumer and criminal justice discourses, both encouraged by economic deregulation and constrained by legislative change, indicative of the ambiguities at the heart of British alcohol policy (25).

The alcohol industry has been shown to have a total operating profit of 26 billion dollars in 2005 (26). The ten largest alcoholic beverage marketers accounted for 48% of the sales (by volume) of globalised brands in 2005. All ten of these are beer companies (27). Globalisation in the alcoholic beverage industry tends to lead to greater concentration of ownership and greater dependence on marketing (27). As a recent study of multinational survival in the global alcohol industry concluded, 'in non-science-based industries such as alcoholic beverages, brands and marketing knowledge rather than technological innovation are central in explaining the growth and survival of multinational firms' (27, 28). An epidemiological cascade model has been developed based on Jahiel's corporation-induced disease theory (29–32) linking economic and political factors to alcohol harms. This model posits that business and political activities of alcohol industry actors are key underlying drivers of alcohol-related harms, and as such require interventions in order to reduce population-level harms (31, 32). Furthermore, McCambridge et al. argue that there is a high degree of collaboration in political strategy development between companies, facilitated by growing concentration among global producers operating in increasingly oligopolistic markets (32).

What do we mean by public health?

There are many definitions of public health including the Acheson definition that states that 'Public health is the science and art of preventing disease, prolonging life and promoting health through organized efforts of society' (33). The World Health Organization (WHO) states that:

> Public health refers to all organized measures (whether public or private) to prevent disease, promote health, and prolong life among the population as a whole. Its activities aim to provide conditions in which people can be healthy and focus on entire populations, not on individual patients or diseases. Thus, public health is concerned with the total system and not only the eradication of a particular disease.
>
> (34)

Public health is therefore a function of the whole of society, to be achieved through the society's 'organized efforts'. Arguably, therefore, a public health system is considered as more inclusive than a health system. Moreover, it is only when different organisations work interactively towards a shared objective, working as a whole, that they can be defined as working as a 'system' (35). We argue that the criminal justice system is a population of its own with many of the population being vulnerable to risk.

The burden of alcohol consumption and crime worldwide

Although alcohol remains to be one of the most commonly used and culturally acceptable substances across the world, according to recent mortality data from the WHO, harmful alcohol consumption directly contributes to over 3 million deaths globally each year (36). Not only does harmful alcohol consumption cause an increased risk of death, but also it is responsible for causing numerous illnesses and diseases across the world, with over 5.1% of the global burden of disease being a direct result of harmful alcohol consumption (36). Alcohol consumption continues to be one of the most prevalent risk factors for premature mortality and disability amongst young people and adults aged between 15 and 49 years, with 10% of all deaths within this age group being caused by harmful alcohol consumption (36). Alcohol consumption is not universal across the world's population, with a clear inequity being observed in alcohol-related illnesses by demographic factors, such as gender and socioeconomic status.

Males are more than three times as likely to suffer from alcohol-related illnesses, with 7.1% of the global burden of diseases in males, caused by the harmful use of alcohol, compared to only 2.2% of females. In addition, individuals from lower socioeconomic groups are disproportionally affected by alcohol, with there being higher rates of alcohol-related death, illness, accidents and injury due to increased consumption across individuals from lower socioeconomic groups (36). It has further been shown that alcohol reduces a person's self-awareness and therefore decreases a person's ability to consider the consequences of their actions (37). Alcohol-induced disinhibition can therefore increase the risk of involvement in violence, whether perpetrating such acts or becoming a victim (38). An alternate explanation relates to reduced cognitive functioning due to acute intoxication, and of executive processing in particular (39).

Alcohol consumption does not only have an impact on the public health of a population but also have wider ramifications for society as a whole. The association between alcohol consumption and crime has long since been observed, with strong evidence confirming a positive correlation between consumption and crime rates (40). Although the relationship between alcohol consumption and crime is often complex, evidence has shown that alcohol use is associated with a large proportion of recorded offences, with prevalent examples including theft, assault, domestic violence, driving under the influence and criminal damage. Some of the common side effects of alcohol consumption, including the lowering of inhibitions, impairing an individual's judgement and the increase in aggressive behaviour, are closely associated with committing criminal offences (41). Examples of this are as follows: in the United States, 35% of victims believe their offenders to be under the influence of alcohol (41). Furthermore, in India, it was found that spousal abuse was 2.5 times more common among individuals consuming alcohol (42). A recent study in Canada, exploring the association between crime and substance use, showed that according to 'an offender's self-report, 42% of all violent and non-violent crime would probably not have occurred if the perpetrator had not been under the influence of, or seeking, alcohol or other substances' (43). By acknowledging the positive correlation between alcohol and crime, predominantly alcohol policies and strategies across the world have included measures to tackle alcohol-related crime. Crime-combating measures typically include reducing the availability of alcohol within an area, enforcing stricter penalties for alcohol-related offences and providing increased access to treatment services and alcohol brief interventions, to attempt to reduce the likelihood of reoffending.

Alcohol use on its own is not a sufficient predictor of aggressive behaviour, considering the severe confounding and effect modification by numerous drinking, personal and contextual variables (44). A large body of international evidence demonstrates a link between alcohol consumption, risky behaviours and criminal activities (45–47). However, because many people who (excessively) drink are not violent, it is tenuous to propose a causal relationship between alcohol and violence where alcohol is a necessary and sufficient cause (44).

Prevalence of alcohol use disorders

A recent worldwide review carried out by Glantz et al. found that alcohol prevalence rates were different across the world (48). They found that mean lifetime prevalence (use) of alcohol use in all countries combined was 80%, ranging from 3.8% to 97.1%. Combined average population lifetime and 12-month prevalence of alcohol use disorders were 8.6% and 2.2% respectively and 10.7% and 4.4% among non-abstainers. Of individuals with a lifetime alcohol use disorder, 43.9% had at least one lifetime mental health disorder and 17.9% of the respondents with a lifetime mental health disorder had a lifetime alcohol use disorder. Alcohol use disorder prevalence was found to be much higher for men than women. Fifteen per cent of all lifetime alcohol use disorder cases developed before age 18. Glantz et al further found that higher household income and being older at time of interview, married and more educated were associated with a lower risk for lifetime alcohol use disorders.

Screening for alcohol use disorders

There are a variety of validated and reliable screening tools available to measure alcohol use disorders including the four-item Cut, Annoyed, Guilty, Eye-opener (CAGE) (49), the Michigan Alcoholism Screening Test (50), the Alcohol, Smoking and Substance Involvement Test (ASSIST) (51) and the Alcohol Use Disorders Identification Test (AUDIT) (52).

The AUDIT is considered to be the gold standard of tools used to identify alcohol use disorders in healthcare settings (52). The ten-question AUDIT is scored between 0 and 40. A score of 8+ for adults indicates an alcohol use disorder, 8–15 indicates hazardous drinking, 16–19 indicates harmful drinking and 20+ indicates probable dependence (22). The AUDIT has been shown to have 92% sensitivity and 94% specificity (22). Furthermore, it has been shown to be effective in the various stages of the criminal justice system (53). Those that score 8 or more are considered to have an alcohol use disorder.

Alcohol brief interventions

Alcohol brief interventions are a secondary prevention activity, which are aimed at those individuals who are drinking in a pattern that is likely to be harmful to their health and/or well-being. Such interventions have been frequently shown to be effective in primary healthcare (54, 55) and there is some evidence in hospital settings (56, 57), but they are typically delivered by practitioners who are not addiction specialists to non-treatment, opportunistic populations (58). Furthermore, there is some evidence of efficacy in regard to reducing recidivism in the criminal justice system (59).

These interventions largely consist of two different approaches: simple structured advice, which, after screening, raises awareness through provision of personalised feedback and advice on steps to reduce drinking behaviour and its adverse consequences; and an extended brief intervention, which generally involves behaviour change counselling. Extended brief intervention introduces and evokes change by giving the participant the opportunity to explore their alcohol use, as well as their motivations and strategies for change. Both forms share the common aim of helping people to change drinking behaviour to promote health (58).

There is a wide variation in the duration and frequency of alcohol brief interventions. However, typically they consist of between one and four sessions and are very short in nature (between 5 and 60 minutes) (60). They generally include personalised feedback on alcohol intake in relation to what the recommended limits are, a discussion of both health and social risks, and may include setting personal targets which can include psychological and motivational interviewing (60). One example of this is using the FRAMES (feedback, responsibility, advice, menus, empathy, self-efficacy) approach (58). Alcohol brief interventions are generally delivered in an opportunistic way by practitioners other than addiction specialists in a wide variety of settings (54).

Due to the established links between risky drinking and crime and the costs to society, in both health and social care, it is important to find interventions that are effective. It has been shown that interventions that capitalise on the 'teachable moment' are conducive with behaviour change, where individuals consider their alcohol use within the context of their offending behaviour and its punitive consequences (61, 62). However, to date, there is a dearth of evidence relating to alcohol use disorders and the use of brief interventions in the criminal justice system (24, 63).

There are barriers in practitioners carrying out alcohol brief interventions (55). These barriers include lack of time, training and resources; a belief that patients will not take advice to change drinking behaviour; and a fear amongst practitioners of offending patients by discussing alcohol (64–66).

The criminal justice system

Crowder et al. states that:

> The criminal justice system is the network of government and private agencies intended to manage accused and convicted criminals. The criminal justice system is comprised of multiple interrelated pillars, consisting of academia, law enforcement, forensic services, the judiciary, and corrections. Legal justice is the result of forging the rights of individuals with the government's corresponding duty to ensure and protect those rights – referred to as due process. These constitutional entitlements cannot be given and protected without the abiding commitments of those professionals working in the criminal justice system. Consequently, such professionals must submit themselves to the ethical principles of the

criminal justice system and evidence persistent integrity in their character. This is accomplished with the help of a worthy code of professional ethics that signals competence, reliability, accountability, and overall trustworthiness – when properly administered.

(67)

Crowder et al. further emphasises the link between public safety and public health with the two being intertwined. He states that 'Public safety issues infer reduced behaviors among offenders and former offenders that place the safety of the public at risk' (67).

Crime statistics

The USA has the highest prisoner rate in the world with around 639 prisoners per 100,000 of the national population (68). The USA also had the largest number of prisoners, at around 2.12 million incarcerated in 2020 (68). African Americans make up the largest share of prisoners in US prisons. In 2018, there were almost 409,600 black, non-Hispanic prisoners compared to 394,800 white, non-Hispanic prisoners (68). Drug-related offenses are the most common cause of imprisonment followed by felonies such as murder and robbery (68).

In England and Wales there were 6,175,738 crimes recorded in 2020 and 6,091,991 in 2021 (69). Around a third of crimes in each year were for violent offences (Table 1.1). Although it is important to note that the total crimes recorded reduced by around 10% during the COVID-19 pandemic (70).

TABLE 1.1 Recorded crime 2020 and 2021 in England and Wales

	2020	% of total – 2020	2021	% of total – 2021
Anti-social behaviour	1,725,849	27.95	1,358,157	22.52
Burglary	277,227	4.49	235,782	3.91
Robbery	61,772	1.00	55,653	0.92
Vehicle	343,954	5.57	321,355	5.33
Violence	1,816,018	29.41	2,029,833	33.66
Shoplifting	241,533	3.91	238,531	3.96
Criminal damage and arson	462,811	7.49	468,174	7.76%
Other theft	351,628	5.69	368,045	6.10
Drugs	186,731	3.02	167,060	2.77
Bike theft	72,977	1.18%	66,673	1.11
Theft from the person	57,254	0.93	65,884	1.09
Weapons	40,939	0.66	41,162	0.68
Public order	436,170	7.06	512,337	8.50
Other crime	100,875	1.63	101,345	1.68
Total	6,175,738		6,029,991	

TABLE 1.2 The crime funnel

Point in the criminal justice system	Number	% of all crime
Crimes experienced by the public	1,000	
Reported to police	530	53.00
Recorded by police	429	42.90
Detected offences	99	9.90
Prosecuted in court	60	6.00
Found/pleaded guilty	50	5.00
Custodial sentence	5	0.50

Data tell us that for every 1,000 crimes experienced by the public, around half are reported to police whilst only 60 (6%) are prosecuted in court (71) (Table 1.2). This shows that the vast majority of crimes are not detected (72). Furthermore, the majority of crimes are committed by a few people, identified as the felonious few as distinct from the miscreant many (73).

Adapted from Ratcliffe (71)

As can be seen in Table 1.2 the funnel of crime statistics shows that the majority of crimes are not prosecuted. Furthermore, more work is needed in how we count crime. If we include all crimes as a count, it does not take into account the severity of crime and looks at all crimes as equal (74). Counting crime has been shown to be difficult and hard to interpret in ways that are needed. Sherman and colleagues argue that the best way to count crime is to assign a weight to the harm caused by each crime, rather than by counting all crimes as if they were created equal (74).

Gender and ethnicity differences in relation to crime

In the UK, men are six times as likely to be arrested as women. There are, on average, around 20 arrests for every 1,000 men and three arrests for every 1,000 women (75). In terms of ethnicity, in the UK, black people are over three times as likely to be arrested as white people. There are, on average, around 29 arrests for every 1,000 black people compared to 9 arrests for every 1,000 white people (75). It has been shown that black men are over three times as likely to be arrested as white men. There are on average 54 arrests for every 1,000 black men and 15 arrests for every 1,000 women (75).

Data from the USA shows that although black people make up 13% of the US population, they make up 33% of persons arrested for non-fatal violent crime, which includes rape, robbery, aggravated assault and other assaults. Black people were 36% of those arrested for serious non-fatal violent crimes, including rape, robbery and aggravated assault (76).

Cost

Adjusting for omission of cost components, the economic costs of alcohol consumption is estimated to amount to 1,306 Int$ per adult (95% confidence interval [CI]: 873–1738), or 2.6% (95% CI: 2.0–3.1%) of the gross domestic product. About one-third of costs (38.8%) are incurred through direct costs, while the majority of costs were due to losses in productivity (61.2%) (77). In England and Wales, alcohol-related crime is estimated to cost society £11.4 billion per year (78). Effective interventions therefore have the potential to significantly reduce the costs relating to substance use, as well as increase individual social welfare (79).

Research shows that around 3.5% of all alcohol-attributable costs in high-income countries are associated with direct law enforcement (5). It is important to note that it is not just alcohol-related crimes but excessive alcohol consumption that plays a role in many other offences, particularly violence and public order offences (80). Evidence shows that victims perceiving offenders to be under the influence of alcohol when a crime is committed has stayed stable at around 45% (81). Between one-third and one-half of perpetrators had consumed alcohol prior to a violent incident; individual country estimates were 35% in the USA, 44% in South Africa, 45% in England and Wales and 50% in China (82).

What is the evidence for causation in relation to alcohol and crime?

As stated earlier there is indeed a complex interplay between individual and contextual factors and risky drinking behaviours and alcohol-related crimes (4). Indeed, alcohol consumption has been shown to induce disinhibition, which in turn may lead to inappropriate social behaviour, characterised by impaired decision-making, agitation, distorted perceptions of social cues and loss of respectful behaviour (4, 83, 84). It has been shown that alcohol is associated with an increased likelihood of committing as well as being exposed to violent acts (85–87). It has also been shown that alcohol can reduce self-awareness and decrease the consequences of one's actions (85, 88).

This book aims to look at the issue from different lenses.

Chapter summary

This chapter has explored issues in relation to alcohol, criminal justice and public health and the complexities around this. It has provided information on crime and alcohol prevalence and described what we mean by public health. It has shown that although levels of crime coming to justice are low, levels of crime attributable to alcohol are high. The rest of this book will explore the different parts of this complex issue.

References

1. Anderson P, Bendtsen P, Spak F, Reynolds J, Drummond C, Colom J, et al. Improving the delivery of brief interventions for heavy drinking in primary health care: Outcome results of the Optimizing Delivery of Health Care Intervention (OHDIN) five-country cluster randomized factorial trial. Addiction. 2016;111(11):1935–45.

2. GBD 2015 Risk Factors Collaborators. Global, regional, and national age-sex specific mortality for 264 causes of death, 1980–2016: A systematic analysis for the Global Burden of Disease Study 2015. Lancet. 2016;8:1659–724.

3. Office for National Statistics. Crime in England and Wales: Year ending March 2022. Available from: www.ons.gov.uk/peoplepopulationandcommunity/crimeand justice/bulletins/crimeinenglandandwales/yearendingmarch2022

4. Graham L, Parkes T, McAuley A, Doi L. Alcohol problems in the criminal justice system: An opportunity for intervention. Denmark: World Health Organization, Regional Office for Europe; 2012.

5. Rehm J, Mathers C, Popova S, Thavorncharoensap M, Teerawattananon Y, Patra J. Global burden of disease and injury and economic cost attributable to alcohol use and alcohol-use disorders. Lancet. 2009;373:2233–33.

6. DoH. Sensible drinking: The report of an inter-departmental working group. London: Department of Health; 1995.

7. Kontis V, Mathers CD, Rehm J, Stevens GA, Shield KD, Bonita R, et al. Contribution of six risk factors to achieving the 25×25 non-communicable disease mortality reduction target: A modelling study. Lancet. 2014;384(9941):427–37.

8. Fillmore KM, Kerr WC, Bostrom A. Changes in drinking status, serious illness and mortality. Journal of Studies on Alcohol and Drugs. 2003;64(2):278–85.

9. Rehm J, Roerecke M. Reduction of drinking in problem drinkers and all-cause mortality. Alcohol and Alcoholism. 2013;48(4):509–13.

10. Boden J, Fergusson D, Horwood L. Alcohol misuse and violent behavior: Findings from a 30-year longitudinal study. Drug & Alcohol Dependence. 2012;122(1–2):135–41.

11. Richardson A, Budd T. Alcohol, crime and disorder: A study of young adults. Report No.: Home Office Research Study 263. London: Home Office Research, Development and Statistics Directorate; 2003 February.

12. Graham L, Heller-Murphy S, Aitken L, McAuley A. Alcohol problems in a remand Scottish prisoner population. International Journal of Prisoner Health. 2012;8(2):51–9.

13. Lightowlers C, Pina-Sánchez J. Intoxication and assault: An analysis of Crown Court sentencing practices in England and Wales. British Journal of Criminology. 2017;58(1):132–54.

14. Lightowlers C, Elliot M, Tranmer M. The dynamic risk of heavy episodic drinking on interpersonal assault in young adolescence and early adulthood. British Journal of Criminology. 2014;54(6):1207–27.

15. Lightowlers C. Exploring the temporal association between young people's alcohol consumption patterns and violent behavior. Contemporary Drug Problems. 2011;38(2):191–212.

16. Graham K, Homel R. Raising the bar: Preventing aggression in and around bars, pubs and clubs. London: Willan Publishing; 2008.

17. Yeomans H, Critcher C. The demon drink: Alcohol and moral regulation, past and present. In: Blackshaw T (ed.) Routledge handbook of leisure studies. London: Routledge; 2020. pp. 305–15.

18. Gusfield JR. Contested meanings: The construction of alcohol problems. University of Wisconsin Press; 1996.

19. Critcher C, Cree V, Clapton G, Smith M. Commentary: Moral panics, yesterday, today and tomorrow. In: Cree VE, Clapton G, Smith M (eds.) Revisiting moral panics. Policy Press; 2015.

20. Jenkins P. Synthetic panics: The symbolic politics of designer drugs. NYU Press; 1999.

21. Parker H, Aldridge J, Measham F, Haynes P. Illegal leisure: The normalisation of adolescent recreational drug use. Oxford University Press; 1999.

22. Saunders JB, Aasland OG, Babor TF, De La Fuente JR, Grant M. Development of the alcohol use disorders identification test (AUDIT): WHO collaborative project on early detection of persons with harmful alcohol consumption. Addiction. 1993;88(6):791–804.

23. World Health Organization. The role of general practice settings in the prevention and management of the harm done by alcohol. Copenhagen: World Health Organization Regional Office for Europe; 1992.

24. Newbury-Birch D, McGovern R, Birch J, O'Neill G, Kaner H, Sondhi A, et al. A rapid systematic review of what we know about alcohol use disorders and brief interventions in the criminal justice system. International Journal of Prisoner Health. 2016;12(1):57–70.

25. Measham F, Brain K. 'Binge' drinking, British alcohol policy and the new culture of intoxication. Crime, Media, Culture. 2005;1(3):262–83.

26. Databank I. The global drinks market: Impact Databank review and forecast, 2006 edn. New York: M Shanken Communications. 2007.

27. Jernigan DH. The global alcohol industry: An overview. Addiction. 2009;104(s1):6–12.

28. Da Silva Lopes T. The growth and survival of multinationals in the global alcoholic beverages industry. Enterprise & Society. 2003;4(4):592–8.

29. Babor TF, Robaina K. Public health, academic medicine, and the alcohol industry's corporate social responsibility activities. American Journal of Public Health. 2013;103(2):206–14.

30. Jahiel RI, Babor TF. Industrial epidemics, public health advocacy and the alcohol industry: Lessons from other fields. [Editorial]. Addiction. 2007;102(9):1335–9. https://doi.org/10.1111/j.1360-0443.2007.01900.x

31. Jahiel RI. Corporation-induced diseases, upstream epidemiologic surveillance, and urban health. Journal of Urban Health. 2008;85(4):517–31.

32. McCambridge J, Coleman R, McEachern J. Public health surveillance studies of alcohol industry market and political strategies: A systematic review. Journal of Studies on Alcohol and Drugs. 2019;80(2):149–57.

33. Acheson D. Public health in England. The report of the Committee of Inquiry into the Future Development of the Public Health Function. London: HMSO; 1988.

34. Turnock B. Public health. Jones & Bartlett; 2012.

35. Marks L, Hunter D, Alderslade R. Strengthening public health capacity and services in Europe. WHO Publications; 2011.

36. Organisation TWH. Health topics: Alcohol 2022. Available from: www.who.int/health-topics/alcohol#tab=tab_1

37. Wells S, Graham K. Aggression involving alcohol: Relationship to drinking patterns and social context. Addiction. 2003;98(1):33–42.

38. Darke S. The toxicology of homicide offenders and victims: A review. Drug and Alcohol Review. 2010;29(2):202–15.

39. Hoaken PNS, Stewart SH. Drugs of abuse and the elicitation of human aggressive behavior. Addictive Behaviors. 2003;28(9):1533–54.

40. Stockwell T, Zhao J, Marzell M, Gruenewald PJ, Macdonald S, Ponicki WR, et al. Relationships between minimum alcohol pricing and crime during the partial

privatization of a Canadian government alcohol monopoly. Journal of Studies on Alcohol and Drugs. 2015;76(4):628–34.

41. Murphy E. Alcohol, drugs and crime recovered 2022; 2023. Available from: https://recovered.org/uk/addiction/alcohol-drugs-and-crime

42. Eashwar VA, Umadevi R, Gopalakrishnan S. Alcohol consumption in India– An epidemiological review. Journal of Family Medicine and Primary Care. 2020;9(1):49.

43. Young MM, De Moor C, Kent P, Stockwell T, Sherk A, Zhao J, et al. Attributable fractions for substance use in relation to crime. Addiction. 2021;116(11):3198–205.

44. van Amsterdam JGC, Ramaekers JG, Verkes R-J, Kuypers KPC, Goudriaan AE, van den Brink W. Alcohol- and drug-related public violence in Europe. European Journal of Criminology. 2020;17(6):806–25.

45. Barton A. Screening and brief intervention of detainees for alcohol use: A social crime prevention approach to combating alcohol-related crime? Howard Journal of Criminal Justice. 2011;50(1):62–74.

46. Needham M, Gummerum M, Mandeville-Norden R, Rakestrow-Dickens J, Mewse A, Barnes A, et al. Association between three different cognitive behavioral alcohol treatment programs and recidivism rates among male offenders: Findings from the United Kingdom. Alcoholism: Clinical and Experimental Research. 2015;39(6):1100–7.

47. Newbury-Birch D, Harrison B, Brown N, Kaner E. Sloshed and sentenced: A prevalence study of alcohol use disorders among offenders in the North East of England. International Journal of Prisoner Health. 2009;5(4):201–11.

48. Glantz MD, Bharat C, Degenhardt L, Sampson NA, Scott KM, Lim CCW, et al. The epidemiology of alcohol use disorders cross-nationally: Findings from the World Mental Health Surveys. Addictive Behaviors. 2020;102:106128.

49. Liskow B, Campbell J, Nickel EJ, Powell BJ. Validity of the CAGE questionnaire in screening for alcohol dependence in a walk-in (triage) clinic. Journal of Studies on Alcohol and Drugs. 1995;56(3):277–81.

50. Selzer ML. The Michigan Alcoholism Screening Test (MAST): The quest for a new diagnostic instrument. American Journal of Psychiatry. 1971;127:1653–8.

51. Humeniuk R, Ali R, Babor TF, Farrell M, Formigoni ML, Jittiwutikarn J, et al. Validation of the alcohol, smoking and substance involvement screening test (ASSIST). Addiction. 2008;103(6):1039–47.

52. Hodgson R, Alwyn T, John B, Thom B, Smith A. The FAST alcohol screening test. Alcohol and Alcoholism. 2002;37(1):61–6.

53. Coulton S, Newbury-Birch D, Cassidy P, Dale V, Deluca P, Gilvarry E, et al. Screening for alcohol use in criminal justice settings: An exploratory study. Alcohol and Alcoholism. 2012;47(4):423–7.

54. Kaner EFS, Beyer FR, Muirhead C, Campbell F, Pienaar ED, Bertholet N, et al. Effectiveness of brief alcohol interventions in primary care populations. Cochrane Database of Systematic Reviews. 2018;2(2):CD004148.

55. O'Donnell A, Kaner E, Newbury-Birch D, Schulte B, Schmidt C, Reimer J, et al. The impact of brief interventions in primary healthcare: A systematic review of reviews. Alcohol and Alcoholism. 2014;49(1):66–78.

56. McQueen J, Howe T, Allan L, Mains D. Brief interventions for heavy alcohol users admitted to general hospital wards. Cochrane Database of Systematic Reviews. 2009;3: CD005191. doi: 10.1002/14651858.CD005191.pub2

57. Gaume J, Bertholet N, McCambridge J, Magill M, Adam A, Hugli O, et al. Effect of a novel brief motivational intervention for alcohol-intoxicated young adults in the emergency department: A randomized clinical trial. JAMA Network Open. 2022;5(10): e2237563.

58. Miller W, Rollnick S. Motivational interviewing; preparing people to change addictive behavior. New York: Guildford Press; 1991.

59. Newbury-Birch D, Coulton S, Bland M, Cassidy P, Dale V, Deluca P, et al. Alcohol screening and brief interventions for offenders in the probation setting (SIPS Trial): A pragmatic multicentre cluster randomised controlled trial. Alcohol and Alcoholism. 2014;49(5):540–8.

60. Haighton CA, Newbury-Birch D, Kaner EFS. Screening and interventions in medical settings including brief feedback-focused interventions. In: Miller P. (ed.) Interventions for addiction: Comprehensive Addictive Behaviors and Disorders. Elsevier Inc., San Diego: Academic Press, 2013. pp. 287–98. ISBN: 9780123983381

61. Babor TF, Grant M. From clinical research to secondary prevention: International collaboration in the development of the alcohol use disorders identification test (AUDIT). Alcohol and Health Research World. 1989;13:371–4.

62. Haighton C, Newbury-Birch D, Durlik C, Sallis A, Chadbourn T, Porter L, et al. Optimising Making Every Contact Count (MECC) interventions: A strategic behavioural analysis. Health Psychology. 2021;40(12):960–73.

63. Newbury-Birch D, Ferguson J, Landale S, Giles EL, McGeechan GJ, Gill C, et al. A systematic review of the efficacy of alcohol interventions for incarcerated people. Alcohol and Alcoholism. 2018;53(4):412–25.

64. Kaner E. Brief alcohol intervention: Time for translational research. Addiction. 2010;105:960–1.

65. Gual A, Sabadini MdA. Implementing alcohol disorders treatment throughout the community. Current Opinion in Psychiatry. 2011;24: 203–7.

66. Anderson P, Wojnar M, Jakubcyk A, Gual A, Segura L, Sovinova H, et al. Managing alcohol problems in General Practice in European OHDIN Survey of General Practitioners. Alcohol and Alcoholism. 2014;49(5):531–9.

67. Crowder S, Turvey BE. Chapter 1 – Ethics in the criminal justice professions. In: Turvey BE, Crowder S (eds.) Ethical justice. San Diego: Academic Press; 2013. pp. 1–19.

68. Statista. *Crime Worldwide – Statistics & Facts 2022*. Available from: www.statista.com/topics/780/crime/#dossierContents__outerWrapper

69. UKCrimeStats. National picture – All crime types and ASB totals. London: UKCrimeStats; 2022. Available from: www.ukcrimestats.com/National_Picture/

70. Home Office. Crime statistics 2020–2021. London: Office for National Statistics. 2021.

71. Ratcliffe J. Reducing crime. A companion for police leaders. Routledge; 2019.

72. Sherman LW. The power few: Experimental criminology and the reduction of harm. Journal of Experimental Criminology. 2007;3(4):299–321.

73. Sherman L, Bland M, House P, Strang H. The felonious few vs. the miscreant many. Cambridge: Cambridge Centre for Evidence Based Policing. 2016.

74. Sherman LW, Associates A. How to count crime: The Cambridge Harm Index Consensus. Cambridge Journal of Evidence-Based Policing. 2020;4:1–14.

75. Gov.UK. Arrests London 2022. Available from: www.ethnicity-facts-figures.service.gov.uk/crime-justice-and-the-law/policing/number-of-arrests/latest

76. Prison Legal News. U.S. DOJ Statistics on race and ethnicity of violent crime perpetrators USA2021. Available from: www.prisonlegalnews.org/news/2021/jun/1/us-doj-statistics-race-and-ethnicity-violent-crime-perpetrators/

77. Manthey J, Hassan SA, Carr S, Kilian C, Kuitunen-Paul S, Rehm J. What are the economic costs to society attributable to alcohol use? A systematic review and modelling study. PharmacoEconomics. 2021;39(7):809–22.

78. Commission on Alcohol Harm. 'It's everywhere' – Alcohol's public face and private hard. UK; 2020.

79. Raistrick D, Heather N, Godfrey C. Review of the effectiveness of treatment for alcohol problems. National Treatment Agency for Substance Misuse, UK. 2006.

80. Flatley J, Kershaw C, Smith K, Chaplin R, Moon D. Crime in England and Wales 2009/10. London: Home Office; 2010.

81. Kershaw C, Nicholas S, Walker A. Crime in England and Wales 2007/2008. London: Home Office Statistical Bulletin; 2008.

82. WHO. Global health risks: Mortality and burden of disease attributable to selected major risk. Geneva: World Health Organization; 2009.

83. Leonard K. Alcohol consumption and escalatory aggression in intoxicated and sober dyads. Journal of Studies on Alcohol and Drugs. 1984;45:75–80.

84. Newbury-Birch D, White M, Kamali F. Factors influencing alcohol and illicit drug use amongst medical students. Drug and Alcohol Dependence. 2000;59:125–30.

85. Darke S. The toxicology of homicide offenders and victims: A review. Drug and Alcohol Review. 2010;29:202–15.

86. Boles SM, Miotto K. Substance abuse and violence: A review of the literature. Aggression and Violent Behavior. 2003;8(2):155–74.

87. Ellickson PL, Tucker JS, Klein DJ. Ten-year prospective study of public health problems associated with early drinking. Pediatrics. 2003;111(5):949–55.

88. Newbury-Birch D, Gilvarry E, McArdle P, Stewart S, Walker J, Lock C, et al. The impact of alcohol consumption on young people: A review of reviews. Department of Children Schools and Families; 2009.

2

THE POLICY CONTEXT OF ALCOHOL AND CRIME

Gillian Waller

Worldwide alcohol policies

The restriction of alcohol and more specifically alcohol policies have been in place across the world for over 3,000 years (1). Despite the fact that alcohol consumption has been recognised as a critical determinant to health, society and the prevalence of crime across the world, the implementation of alcohol policies across the world remains to be highly variable. A study, conducted in 2007 by Brand et al., looked at determining whether there was an association observed between a country having a strict alcohol policy and the alcohol consumption across that country's population (1). Brand et al. found that, across the 30 countries included in the sample, a clear inverse relationship between policy strength and alcohol consumption was present, as when an alcohol policy was stricter, alcohol consumption decreased (1). Although the study argued that having a strict alcohol policy was not the sole contributor to alcohol consumption within a country and it is likely to include a plethora of other variables and cultural norms, it does offer evidence for policy strength being one of the factors negatively affecting alcohol consumption (1).

Alcohol policy in Norway

An example of a group of countries with extremely restrictive alcohol policies in place is the Nordic countries, which currently have some of the strictest alcohol restrictions in the world (2). In Norway, the access and availability to alcohol is limited by the restriction of opening hours of alcohol retailers, and there are strict restrictions on where, when and to whom alcohol can be served (2). The COVID-19 pandemic in 2020 caused a monumental shift in daily life across the world and unsurprisingly had a significant impact on alcohol policy. During the pandemic,

DOI: 10.4324/9781003169802-2

alcohol consumption was even more restricted in Norway, with the serving of alcohol being completely prohibited twice during the year of 2020 (3). A study by Gerell et al., exploring the impact of these alcohol bans on criminal offences, found that the restrictions and bans on serving alcohol were seen to reduce crime, although there were no discernible patterns by the type of crime or the time of day (3). Similar reductions in crime, as a result of the banning or restriction of alcohol sales during the COVID-19 lockdowns, were also reported in African countries, such as Namibia and Madagascar, and in South Africa, where there was reported to be a significant decline in alcohol-related violence (4).

However, in contrast, the study by Gerell et al. also found that when pubs or licensed establishments were ordered to not serve alcohol after midnight, the level of crime recorded increased (3). Therefore, the study provides an example of why it is not always intuitive to have an extremely restrictive alcohol policy, when the focus is to reduce alcohol-related crime.

Although, as previously discussed, alcohol consumption is a global concern, the context of alcohol consumption varies by country, and hence unsurprisingly there is heterogeneity observed around alcohol consumption levels, cultural norms and alcohol-related crime levels. Consequently, it would be counter-intuitive to expect to have a one-size-fits-all policy that would be able to be universally implemented across the world. However, the World Health Organization (WHO) sought to develop an alcohol initiative that had salience and relevance globally, by using the best placed evidence, in order to provide a series of alcohol interventions that could have broad applicability.

The WHO is an organisation dedicated to improving international health, by making use of the most up-to-date evidence and guidance and working directly with partners to lead global health responses. After comprehensive development and collaborative work with international colleagues, the WHO launched the SAFER alcohol initiative in 2018. The SAFER initiative consists of five specific alcohol interventions, which were developed as a result of the evidence around alcohol-related harm and its impact on health and society (5).

SAFER is an acronym for:

S: Strengthen restrictions on alcohol availability,
A: Advance and enforce drink-driving countermeasures,
F: Facilitate access to screening, brief interventions and treatment,
E: Enforce bans or comprehensive restrictions on alcohol advertising, sponsorship or promotion and,
R: Raise prices on alcohol through excise taxes and pricing policies (5).

Making alcohol less available through laws, policies and programmes, making alcohol recovery treatment more widespread and increasing the cost of alcohol, are all ways to reduce the harms associated with alcohol and would thereby support in the reduction of alcohol-related offences. The five SAFER interventions have been valuable in informing the development and implementation of alcohol policies and restrictions across the world.

Alcohol policy and crime in Canada and the USA

By considering the strength of alcohol policy and the association with crime, in both the USA and Canada, it invokes certain similarities. In Canada, alcohol consumption has steadily declined over the last decade, but alcohol still remains to be one of the most commonly used recreational substances and alcohol sales were observed to have increased in the year 2019 (6). The legalisation of cannabis in Canada in 2018 saw the implementation of extensive regulations, which supported the regulated and restricted access to cannabis. Despite the strict restrictions being introduced around cannabis use, the policies associated with alcohol consumption remain to be variable across Canada and the implementation of the best established evidence remains to be inconsistent (6). A recent study by Vallance et al. looked to determine the magnitude of the problem by scoring different Canadian provinces' alcohol policies by their scope and effectiveness (6). The implementation score was shown to vary significantly and ranged from 38.4% in the Northwest Territories to 63.9% in Ontario, suggesting there is a significant room for improvement within the scope and the effectiveness of alcohol policies across Canada (6).

Professor Tim Stockwell has been a leading and influential driver of change within the alcohol and public policy field in Canada. His work in championing and evaluating minimum alcohol pricing (7–10) has been instrumental in the implementation of minimum alcohol pricing across the world, including in Scotland, which will be discussed later in this chapter. Making alcohol less affordable, by increasing the lowest price for alcohol or introducing a minimum price per gram of alcohol, is considered to be a key weapon in the arsenal when aiming to reduce alcohol-related harm (7). A systematic review, by Wagenaar et al., which explored the association between increased alcohol taxation and morbidity and mortality, found that often health and social outcomes are improved substantially when alcohol is more expensive (11). This was supported by an observed decrease in alcohol-related crime, such as reduced rates of alcohol-related violence and less incidences of driving under the influence of alcohol (11).

Across the years, multiple studies by Stockwell and colleagues have explored how the increase in alcohol prices, in British Columbia, Canada, has affected the prevalence of alcohol-related crime (9). Their study in 2017 highlighted that, following the introduction of increased minimum alcohol prices, the number of recorded alcohol-related, traffic-related and violent crimes perpetrated by men was seen to decrease (12). In addition, increasing the cost of alcohol was also shown to be associated with a reduction in acute and chronic alcohol-related hospital admissions (8). Stockwell and his colleagues have also been involved in exploring the use of government monopolies for the sale and distribution of alcohol (13). Government alcohol monopolies have been used across the world to regulate the sales of alcohol, in order to minimise the health and social challenges associated with alcohol consumption (13). However, they can also have negative connotations when they are used to prioritise monetary gains, but in general they do provide another way in which public health and population indicators can be improved (14)

Similar to Canada, the US alcohol policies vary by state in their restrictions and implementation and there has been a large body of research undertaken exploring how the impact of a state's alcohol policy can affect public health outcomes and the rates of crime. An example of this is the study by Naimi et al. in 2018 which sought to determine whether there was an association between the restrictiveness of a state's alcohol policy and the probability of alcohol being a factor in the occurrence of fatalities, via a motor vehicle crash (15). A state's alcohol policy was rated by the research team using a developed Alcohol Policy Scale (APS). The study found that 'a 10–percentage point increase in the restrictiveness of the state alcohol policy environment was associated with a 10% reduced odds that a crash fatality was alcohol related' (15).

A second example of this is the study by Lira et al. which looked to determine the relationship between a US state's alcohol policies and the alcohol involvement among victims of intimate partner homicide (16). As previously discussed, alcohol consumption continues to be a significant risk factor for violence and homicide, particularly within domestic partners. The results of the study indicated that alcohol use was more prevalent among victims of intimate partner homicide, and states, which had implemented a more-restrictive alcohol policy, were associated with reduced odds of alcohol-related homicides (16).

The UK: An alcohol policy case study

Alcohol consumption in the UK has continued to be amongst the highest in the world causing a huge burden on the UK population's health and society. Around 21% of adults in England and 24% in England and Scotland regularly consume alcohol at levels that increase their risk of ill health (17). The availability and the affordability of alcohol in the UK have increased over the years, resulting in significant alcohol-related harm (18). The National Health Service (NHS) faces ever-increasing pressure from alcohol-related illnesses, including liver diseases such as cirrhosis, and a plethora of different cancers alongside alcohol-related accidents and injuries (19). Economic hardship and consistent cuts to public funding have resulted in the reduced availability of community alcohol and addiction services and less resources have been assigned to local public health teams who are responsible for developing alcohol strategies and services within their area (19).

According to a report, published by Public Health England in 2019, approximately one in five people is harmed by another person's alcohol consumption (19). An example of this 'second-hand harm' could include being a victim of alcohol-related crime (19) and in England and Wales it has been estimated that two in five violent incidents are alcohol related (20, 21). Unsurprisingly, therefore, alcohol-related violent crime in England presents a monumental challenge, with it costing the police and criminal justice system in excess of £1.6 billion per year (20). Alcohol-related crime also contributes to the overburdening of the NHS, as it is often associated with injuries and hence puts more pressure on the accident and emergency services (20). Consequently, due to the monumental strain on resources, alcohol consumption poses in the UK; it is interesting to consider the landscape and policy context surrounding alcohol in the UK and what strategies have been implemented over the last 20 years in order to reduce alcohol-related harm.

The Alcohol Harm Reduction Strategy of England, 2004

Alcohol consumption in the UK peaked in the year 2004, where adults, aged 15 years or over, on average were observed to be drinking 9.5 litres of pure alcohol per year (22). This led to the government producing the long-awaited Alcohol Harm Reduction Strategy of England (AHRSE) (23). The AHRSE was introduced as a way in which to recognise the extent of the alcohol problems within England, and to provide guidance around how to reduce the harms associated with alcohol consumption, both to an individual's health and to society as a whole (18, 23, 24). Due to the relative increase in alcohol affordability over the previous decades, unsurprisingly leading to a sharp increase in alcohol consumption, a new strategy was needed to tackle it. The AHRSE focused around four key objectives: education and information, better identification of problem and treatment, reducing alcohol-related crime and the alcohol industry as a voluntary partner (18). The strategy around alcohol-related crime recognised the impact of antisocial behaviour in public places, underage drinking, driving under the influence of alcohol and alcohol-related violence. It set out measures to tackle the increase in alcohol-related crime, which came with the increase in alcohol consumption across the population. Measures included the introduction of individual fines, conditional cautions and implementing antisocial behaviour orders for repeat offenders of alcohol-related crime (18).

However, the AHRSE was not as extensive as originally hoped and hence was met with intense criticism and was labelled as 'a missed opportunity and incapable of implementation' (25). Even though the AHRSE recognised the importance of reducing alcohol consumption, the strategy did not document any practical measures to restrict alcohol availability, increase alcohol taxation, to reduce affordability and the government did not allocate any additional financial means to implement the strategy (18, 24). In addition, a significant failing of the AHRSE was that it was believed to have received substantial funding and hence influence from the alcohol industry (18). Therefore, the AHRSE was deemed to be ineffective and swift action was needed to reverse peak in alcohol consumption in the UK and alleviate the concerns to public health and society (18, 24).

Alcohol marketing rules, 2004

During the same year as the AHRSE, new guidelines around alcohol marketing were introduced in the UK to ameliorate the power of alcohol advertising. As previously discussed, alcohol consumption had peaked in the UK in 2004 and prior to this, alcohol advertising was prolific and wholly unregulated across media, television, online and event sponsoring. There has been comprehensive evidence documenting the positive correlation between alcohol marketing and an increase in alcohol consumption (26, 27). For this reason, rules were introduced in 2004 by the Advertising Standards Agency (ASA) and Ofcom, the regulating bodies within the UK, which sought to restrict alcohol marketing (28, 29).

As it currently stands, the UK alcohol advertising rules are amongst the strictest in the world (28). A substantial focus of the alcohol advertising marketing rules was focused around protecting young people from alcohol marketing, and hence underage acquisition of alcohol (28). This is due to the fact that young people are at a significantly greater risk of alcohol-related harm, compared to adults and it is a criminal offence for young people, aged under 18 years, to access alcohol (30). In the UK it is illegal for young people, aged under 18 years, to purchase alcohol in any retailers or licensed premises (31). In addition, it is illegal for adults to purchase alcohol for young people, unless the young person is 16 or 17 years of age and it is beer, wine or cider with a meal (31).

Not only does harmful alcohol consumption have health impacts on young people, but young people who consume alcohol regularly are more likely to be involved in crime and antisocial behaviour. Although there is a plethora of contributory factors to a young person's offending behaviour, substance use, including alcohol consumption, is commonly associated with increased risk-taking behaviour such as committing crimes (32). In a recent study by Hammerton et al., it reported that strong associations existed between 'early-onset persistent' conduct problems and adolescent alcohol consumption, and criminal behaviour and alcohol-related problems, in young people aged 18 years (33). Due to the intense threat alcohol consumption poses to young people and hence their behaviour, alcohol consumption in young people within the criminal justice system will be explored in greater depth in Chapter 6.

Returning to alcohol marketing, research evidence has consistently shown that exposure to alcohol marketing is associated with earlier drinking initiation in young people and higher alcohol consumption, such as binge and hazardous drinking (34). Therefore, the ASA and Ofcom in the UK introduced advertising rules applicable across all media to regulate alcohol marketing in young people (28, 29). The rules included 'alcohol adverts should not be targeted at young people, aged under 18, or include any material relevant to a young person or their popular culture' (28, 29). Alcohol adverts must not appear in programmes targeted at audiences under 18 years and the actors or actresses featured in the adverts must be over 25 years of age and look their age (28, 29).

Other ageless rules around alcohol marketing were introduced to ensure protection of all individuals. These include ensuring that alcohol is not marketed in an irresponsible way including no reference to binge drinking or alcohol being served irresponsibly, not portraying alcohol consumption as being a challenge or with tough or daring behaviour, alcohol not being used to increase popularity, sexual success or an individual's confidence or being used for therapeutic purposes (28, 29).

Safe. Sensible. Social, 2007

In 2007, the next alcohol strategy 'Safe. Sensible. Social.' was produced by the Department of Health in England, succeeding AHRSE (35). It aimed to clearly set out what is acceptable or sensible alcohol consumption, in order to protect individuals, families and communities from harm (35). One of the main strengths of Safe. Sensible. Social was that it recognised the importance of targeting specific groups within the population, who were most at risk from alcohol consumption and those most at risk of consuming alcohol at harmful levels. It provided guidelines for parents and young people around what are safe and sensible limits for young people (35). It also acknowledged that the greatest increase in alcohol-related deaths and ill health was within males, aged between 35 and 54 years, and hence they should be a key group in which alcohol interventions and support should be targeted at (24). In regards to alcohol and crime, the strategy continued to maintain a focus around reducing alcohol-related violence, specifically focusing on penalties for binge-drinkers who were responsible for the most alcohol-related offences (35).

However, similarly to AHRSE, Safe. Sensible. Social was problematic as it gave a heavy focus to the alcohol-related offending and actions recognised through the Drinkaware Trust, which is exclusively funded by the alcohol industry (24).

The UK Government's Alcohol Strategy, 2012

Following the failure of the AHRSE and Safe. Sensible. Social. Strategies to evoke significant change in the alcohol policy arena, the latest Government's Alcohol Strategy was released in 2012, which was developed using the most up-to-date evidence in the field (36). It was quickly viewed as '*a landmark piece of work and the single biggest policy change in the alcohol landscape for a considerable time*' (37). The Government's Alcohol Strategy proposed that '*fast, immediate action, where universal change is needed*' to reduce the harms perpetuated by the rising levels of alcohol consumption. It predominantly focused on the need to eliminate the UK's 'binge drinking' culture, which was particularly topical as in 2012, binge drinking accounted for over half of the alcohol consumed within the UK, and was seen to cause a substantial burden to healthcare services and society. Another specific target of the strategy was to reduce the alcohol-related violence and disorder, which can be observed across different communities and families, specifically young people and children.

Specific measures to tackle alcohol-related harm within the strategy were to elicit consultations around a minimum unit price for alcohol, banning the sale of multi-buy alcohol discounting and to introduce stronger measures to control the density of local licensed premises (36). It is recognised that the affordability of alcohol in the UK has dramatically increased over the past decades, and therefore 'cheap' alcohol remains to be affordable across the population (36). It also acknowledged the need to tackle the increased numbers of the population drinking harmful levels of alcohol at home, before then going on a night out, which was labelled as 'pre-loading' (36). Pre-loading was deemed to be harmful as it not only has increased health risks to the individual by consuming larger quantities of alcohol, but it was also positively associated with alcohol-related violence (36). Evidence showed that individuals who engaged in pre-loading, before they went out, were two and a half times more likely to be involved in violence than those who didn't (36). In regards to measures to reduce crime and alcohol-related crime, the strategy proposed the exploration of innovative sobriety schemes, which would aim to challenge alcohol-related offending and offenders (36).

Generally, the strategy was received more positively than the previous AHRSE and Safe. Sensible. Social as it was deemed to be informed by the most up-to date evidence, whilst incorporating the learning from alcohol guidance across the world (38). It proposed discussions around the introduction of minimum price per gram of alcohol, which has been successfully introduced in other countries, and the strategy also looked at superseding previously ineffective attempts of decreasing the availability of alcohol (36). However, the strategy did have weaker areas and one of those was identified was the fact that it had a greater focus on crime reduction, opposed to a public health focus (37). Although, as contextualised in this chapter, the two areas are often inextricably linked, experts in the field talked about the strategy and its failure to move away from alcohol being seen as just a criminal justice issue, rather than a health issue (37).

Modern crime prevention strategy, 2016

The latter point was further supported when the Modern Crime Prevention strategy was released in 2016. Although not a specific alcohol strategy, the Modern Crime Prevention Strategy set out a series of alcohol-related, crime objectives (39). The Modern Crime Prevention Strategy was developed to capitalise on updates to the existing evidence, in order to consider new strategies for crime prevention (39). Despite the fact that crime generally was seen to be decreasing in the UK, over the last 20 years prior to the strategy release; the crimes recorded had been observed to be changing, with a large shift towards online fraud and cybercrime (39). In addition, the consumption of alcohol and other substances continued to be a key driver of crime in the UK. The strategy stated that in approximately half of all violent incidents recorded, the victim believed the offender(s) to be under the influence of alcohol, at the time of the offence (39). That was seen to be more prolific in incidents occurring between strangers and in offences in the evening, at weekends and in public places (39).

Although, as previously discussed, the relationship between alcohol and crime is complex, the association was acknowledged as being indisputable, and thereby the strategy set out to outline measures to reduce alcohol consumption and alcohol-related crime and disorder. Key actions included improving the local intelligence around the decisions on the sale of alcohol, establishing effective local partnerships with the management of the night-time alcohol economy and equipping the police and local authorities with the authority and knowledge to promote swift and decisive action, around alcohol crime and disorder (39). A definitive area that was included within the strategy was the importance of influencing alcohol consumption, through individual behaviour change, across the population (39). This was proposed via the exploration of providing brief alcohol interventions, outside of a traditional healthcare setting and which included both the offenders and the victims of crime (39). The strategy also proposed the adoption of a life-course approach, with a range of available alcohol treatment. This was defined as seeking to prevent the initial onset of risky alcohol consumption and its escalation, by providing universal support across the population and enhanced support, targeted towards the most at-risk, vulnerable individuals (39).

Minimum unit pricing in Scotland, 2018

Scotland, a country within the UK, implemented the alcohol Minimum Unit Pricing (MUP) policy in 2018, following on from the success of introducing a minimum alcohol price in other countries (8). Scotland at the time has significantly higher rates of alcohol consumption, in comparison to England and Wales; with one in four adults (24%) in Scotland being seen to consume alcohol at hazardous or harmful levels (defined as consuming more than 14 units per week) (40). Therefore, in 2018, the Scottish Government released the 'Rights, Respect and Recovery: Alcohol and Drug Treatment strategy', which was compiled to improve health by preventing and reducing alcohol and drug use and the related harms (41). One of their key initiatives prior to introducing the strategy to improve alcohol-related harm was to introduce MUP.

The R of the WHO's SAFER alcohol initiative (5) set out that, by raising the prices on alcohol, it decreases the availability of alcohol across a population. MUP for alcohol was introduced in Scotland on 1 May 2018 (42). It was brought in to legislate that all drinks containing alcohol should have a minimum price of £0.50 per unit of alcohol and therefore should not legally be sold for a price lower than that (42). The more units of alcohol a drink contains, the more expensive the MUP will be. The rationale behind the introduction of MUP was to ensure that alcoholic drinks were being sold at consistent and sensible prices (42). Making alcohol unaffordable is deemed by the WHO to be one of the best ways to prevent alcohol-related harm (5, 43). One of the key impacts of MUP was raising the cost of the cheapest, shop-bought alcohol. Often individuals, who are chronically abusing alcohol, particularly those in low-income groups, favour low-cost, high-strength alcohol. By increasing the cost of these alcoholic drinks and setting an alcohol MUP across the board, the policy aimed to save lives, reduce alcohol-associated illnesses and injuries, whilst having a positive on society, including the reduction of crime, offending and re-offending (42).

Following the first year of implementation, the Monitoring and Evaluating Scotland's Alcohol Strategy (MESAS) report in 2019 was compiled, which set out to determine the impact of the alcohol strategy in Scotland. It found that alcohol sales in Scotland decreased by 3% in 2018, in direct contrast to a 2% increase in alcohol sales in England (44). Further work saw a modelling exercise identifying that alcohol MUP was associated with a reduction in weekly alcohol purchases of 9.5g per adult, per household (44).

Although these early indications of the implementation of MUP looked positive, a recent study has indicated that individuals in lower income groups, specifically younger men, which were one of the key targets of MUP, were not seen to reduce their alcohol use (45). In addition, an evaluation into the impact of alcohol MUP on crime found that the long-term decline in all recorded crime and disorder had ceased prior to the introduction of MUP and hence there appeared to be no change in the rates of alcohol-related crime (46). The most recent MESAS report from 2022 indicates that alcohol sold in the UK was still 78% more affordable than it was in 1987, highlighting that there is still a significant room for improvement (47). Since the introduction of the MUP in Scotland, there has been the unprecedented COVID-19 pandemic in 2020, forcing the population into lockdowns and thus affecting the sales and consumption of alcohol. Therefore, it would be advantageous to continue to evaluate the impact of the implementation of the alcohol MUP, in order to determine its effectiveness at reducing alcohol consumption in Scotland.

Advancing our Health: Prevention in the 2020s

A decade on, although the government announced plans to update the 2012 alcohol strategy in 2018, this did not happen, and thus the 2012 version remains to be the latest full alcohol strategy (48). However, the planned update did not go ahead, due to the release of the most recent Green Paper, entitled 'Advancing our Health: Prevention in the 2020s' which was released in July 2019 (49). Advancing our Health was produced with the aim of introducing the concept of proactive, predictive and personalised prevention, which is characterised by the shifting in focus from treatment, to exploring the ways in which health problems can be prevented in the first place (49). It set out '*intelligent public health*' as a way to tackle some of the biggest health challenges (49). As a fundamental part of this, it contained strategies aimed at reducing alcohol-related harm, due to the fact that alcohol consumption remains to be a key contributor to chronic illnesses, morbidity and mortality. Although alcohol consumption in the UK is now seen to be declining, particularly amongst young people, the harm caused by risky alcohol consumption is rising, due to the prevalence of heavy drinking (49). The heaviest drinkers make up 4% of the population, but account for 30% of all alcohol consumed within the UK (49). Individuals in a low socioeconomic group are disproportionately affected, with the impact of harmful drinking and alcohol dependence being greater for those in the lowest income bracket (49).

Advancing our Health proposed, working directly with industry, to make alcohol-free and low-alcohol products more widely available, in order to allow individuals to have greater choice by being able to access lower strength alternatives (49). In addition, it also set out plans for the NHS, which included the NHS Long Term plan, which also focused around the shift towards prevention, and hence included a package of measures, such as the dedication of funds to establish alcohol care teams in a wider range of areas (49).

Chapter summary

It is clear that when considering the policy context of alcohol, crime and society, across the world there has been considerable progress made and in general, alcohol consumption is declining, especially in young people (50). However, those who do consume alcohol tend to consume larger amounts, at more harmful levels, causing damage to their health and increasing their likelihood of being involved in crime and disorder. Therefore, it is still imperative that alcohol policy and the links to crime remains to be a key consideration of governments across the world. Considering the UK policy context, although numerous strategies have been implemented over the years, including the radical minimum unit policy in Scotland, there are still high levels of alcohol consumption and alcohol-related crime. More needs to be done around incorporating new and innovative ways of addressing alcohol consumption and making use of the most up-to-date evidence in the field.

References

1. Brand DA, Saisana M, Rynn LA, Pennoni F, Lowenfels AB. Comparative analysis of alcohol control policies in 30 countries. PLoS Medicine. 2007;4(4):e151.
2. Li J, Wu B, Tevik K, Krokstad S, Helvik A-S. Factors associated with elevated consumption of alcohol in older adults—Comparison between China and Norway: The CLHLS and the HUNT Study. BMJ Open. 2019;9(8):e028646.
3. Gerell M, Allvin A, Frith M, Skardhamar T. COVID-19 restrictions, pub closures, and crime in Oslo, Norway. Nordic Journal of Criminology. 2022;23:1–20.
4. Matzopoulos R, Walls H, Cook S, London L. South Africa's COVID-19 alcohol sales ban: The potential for better policy-making. International Journal of Health Policy and Management. 2020;9(11):486.
5. WHO. The SAFER initiative – A world free from alcohol-related harm; 2018. Available from: www.who.int/initiatives/SAFER#:~:text=Every%2010%20seco nds%2a%20person,to%20reduce%20alcohol%20related%20harm
6. Vallance K, Stockwell T, Wettlaufer A, Chow C, Giesbrecht N, April N, et al. The Canadian Alcohol Policy Evaluation project: Findings from a review of provincial and territorial alcohol policies. Drug and Alcohol Review. 2021;40(6):937–45.
7. Stockwell T, Zhao J, Giesbrecht N, Macdonald S, Thomas G, Wettlaufer A. The raising of minimum alcohol prices in Saskatchewan, Canada: Impacts on consumption and implications for public health. American Journal of Public Health. 2012;102(12):e103–e110.
8. Stockwell T, Zhao J, Martin G, Macdonald S, Vallance K, Treno A, et al. Minimum alcohol prices and outlet densities in British Columbia, Canada: Estimated impacts on alcohol-attributable hospital admissions. American Journal of Public Health. 2013;103(11):2014–20.

9. Stockwell T, Zhao J, Marzell M, Gruenewald PJ, Macdonald S, Ponicki WR, et al. Relationships between minimum alcohol pricing and crime during the partial privatization of a Canadian government alcohol monopoly. Journal of Studies on Alcohol and Drugs. 2015;76(4):628–34.

10. Stockwell T, Giesbrecht N, Vallance K, Wettlaufer A. Government options to reduce the impact of alcohol on human health: Obstacles to effective policy implementation. Nutrients. 2021;13(8):2846.

11. Wagenaar AC, Tobler AL, Komro KA. Effects of alcohol tax and price policies on morbidity and mortality: A systematic review. American Journal of Public Health. 2010;100(11):2270–8.

12. Stockwell T, Zhao J, Sherk A, Callaghan RC, Macdonald S, Gatley J. Assessing the impacts of Saskatchewan's minimum alcohol pricing regulations on alcohol-related crime. Drug and Alcohol Review. 2017;36(4):492–501.

13. Stockwell T, Sherk A, Norström T, Angus C, Ramstedt M, Andréasson S, et al. Estimating the public health impact of disbanding a government alcohol monopoly: Application of new methods to the case of Sweden. BMC Public Health. 2018;18(1):1–16.

14. Room R, Örnberg JC. Government monopoly as an instrument for public health and welfare: Lessons for cannabis from experience with alcohol monopolies. International Journal of Drug Policy. 2019;74:223–8.

15. Naimi TS, Xuan Z, Sarda V, Hadland SE, Lira MC, Swahn MH, et al. Association of state alcohol policies with alcohol-related motor vehicle crash fatalities among US adults. JAMA Internal Medicine. 2018;178(7):894–901.

16. Lira MC, Xuan Z, Coleman SM, Swahn MH, Heeren TC, Naimi TS. Alcohol policies and alcohol involvement in intimate partner homicide in the US. American Journal of Preventive Medicine. 2019;57(2):172–9.

17. GOV.UK. Guidance Chapter 12: Alcohol. Department of Health and Social Care; 2021. Available from: www.gov.uk/government/publications/delivering-better-oral-health-an-evidence-based-toolkit-for-prevention/chapter-12-alcohol#:~:text=cancer%20(8).-,Alcohol%20consumption,risk%20drinkers)%20(9)

18. Drummond C, Chengappa S. Alcohol industry and alcohol policy in the United Kingdom. Nordic Studies on Alcohol and Drugs. 2006;23(6):487–98.

19. Williams R, Aithal G, Alexander GJ, Allison M, Armstrong I, Aspinall R, et al. Unacceptable failures: The final report of the Lancet Commission into liver disease in the UK. Lancet. 2020;395(10219):226–39.

20. (IAS) IoAS. Alcohol-related violence: A summary of research presented at the 2021 British Society of Criminology Conference; 2022. Available from: www.ias.org.uk/2021/09/01/alcohol-related-violence-a-summary-of-research-presented-at-the-2021-british-society-of-criminology-conference/#:~:text=reduce%20alcohol%20harm-,Alcohol%2Drelated%20violence%3A%20a%20summary%20of%20research%20presented%20at%20the,British%20Society%20of%20Criminology%20conference&text=In%20England%20and%20Wales%2C%20approximately,violent%20incidents%20are%20alcohol%2Drelated

21. Census 2021. The nature of violent crime in England and Wales: Year ending March 2020; 2021. Available from: www.ons.gov.uk/peoplepopulationandcommunity/crimeandjustice/articles/thenatureofviolentcrimeinenglandandwales/yearendingmarch2020

22. Institute of Alcohol Studies (IoAS). Alcohol consumption factsheet; 2017.

23. Unit PMsS. Alcohol harm reduction strategy for England; 2004. Available from: www.ias.org.uk/uploads/pdf/Economic%20impacts%20docs/AlcoholHarmReductionStrategy.pdf

24. Anderson P. A safe, sensible and social AHRSE: New Labour* and alcohol policy. Addiction. 2007;102(10):1515–21.

25. Babor TF. Admirable ends, ineffective means: Comments on the alcohol harm reduction strategy for England. Drugs: Education, Prevention and Policy. 2004;11(5):361–5.

26. Noel JK, Sammartino CJ, Rosenthal SR. Exposure to digital alcohol marketing and alcohol use: A systematic review. Journal of Studies on Alcohol and Drugs, Supplement. 2020;(s19):57–67.

27. Saffer H, Dave D. Alcohol consumption and alcohol advertising bans. Applied Economics. 2002;34(11):1325–34.

28. (ASA) ASA. Alcohol – Helpful information on the advertising rules for alcohol ads and examples of previous Advertising Standards Authority rulings in this area ASA; 2022. Available from: www.asa.org.uk/topic/alcohol.html#:~:text=Alcohol%20 ads%20must%20not%20be,or%20over%2C%20and%20look%20it

29. Ofcom. Final revised alcohol advertising rules; 2004. Available from: www.ofcom. org.uk/__data/assets/pdf_file/0013/28021/rules.pdf

30. Patton R, Deluca P, Kaner E, Newbury-Birch D, Phillips T, Drummond C. Alcohol screening and brief intervention for adolescents: The how, what and where of reducing alcohol consumption and related harm among young people. Alcohol and Alcoholism. 2013;49(2):207–12.

31. GOV.UK. Alcohol and young people: Crown copyright; 2022. Available from: www. gov.uk/alcohol-young-people-law

32. Newbury-Birch D, Jackson K, Hodgson T, Gilvarry E, Cassidy P, Coulton S, et al. Alcohol-related risk and harm amongst young offenders aged 11–17. International Journal of Prisoner Health. 2015;11(2):75–86.

33. Hammerton G, Edwards AC, Mahedy L, Murray J, Maughan B, Kendler KS, et al. Externalising pathways to alcohol-related problems in emerging adulthood. Journal of Child Psychology and Psychiatry. 2020;61(6):721–31.

34. Jernigan D, Noel J, Landon J, Thornton N, Lobstein T. Alcohol marketing and youth alcohol consumption: A systematic review of longitudinal studies published since 2008. Addiction. 2017;112:7–20.

35. HM Government. Safe. Sensible. Social. The next steps in the National Alcohol Strategy; 2007. Available from: www.choiceforum.org/docs/safe.pdf

36. HM Government. The government's alcohol strategy; 2012. Available from: https:// assets.publishing.service.gov.uk/government/uploads/system/uploads/attachment_ data/file/224075/alcohol-strategy.pdf

37. Ward S. The government's alcohol strategy: A view from the both ends of the world. Drugs: Education, Prevention and Policy. 2012;19(5):368–9.

38. Anderson P. The UK government's alcohol strategy. Drugs: Education, Prevention and Policy. 2012;19(5):360–1.

39. Office H. Modern crime prevention strategy; 2016. Available from: https://ass ets.publishing.service.gov.uk/government/uploads/system/uploads/attachment_d ata/file/509831/6.1770_Modern_Crime_Prevention_Strategy_final_WEB_vers ion.pdf

40. Alcohol Focus Scotland. Alcohol facts and figures; 2019. Available from: www.alco hol-focus-scotland.org.uk/alcohol-information/alcohol-facts-and-figures/

41. Scotland Government. Rights, respect and recovery: Alcohol and drug treatment strategy; 2018. Available from: www.gov.scot/publications/rights-respect-recovery/

42. Scotland Government. Alcohol and drugs policy – Minimum unit pricing; 2022. Available from: www.gov.scot/policies/alcohol-and-drugs/minimum-unit-pricing/

43. Anderson P, O'Donnell A, Kaner E, Llopis EJ, Manthey J, Rehm J. Impact of minimum unit pricing on alcohol purchases in Scotland and Wales: Controlled interrupted time series analyses. Lancet Public Health. 2021;6(8):e557–e65.

44. O'Donnell A, Anderson P, Jané-Llopis E, Manthey J, Kaner E, Rehm J. Immediate impact of minimum unit pricing on alcohol purchases in Scotland: Controlled interrupted time series analysis for 2015–18. BMJ. 2019;15274:366.

45. Rehm J, O'Donnell A, Kaner EF, LLopis EJ, Manthey J, Anderson P. Differential impact of minimum unit pricing on alcohol consumption between Scottish men and women: Controlled interrupted time series analysis. BMJ Open. 2022;12(7):e054161.

46. Krzemieniewska-Nandwani K, Bannister J, Ellison M, Adepeju M. Evaluation of the impact of alcohol minimum unit pricing (MUP) on crime and disorder, public safety and public nuisance; 2021. Available from: www.drugsandalcohol.ie/34951/1/evaluation-of-the-impact-of-alcohol-minimum-unit-pricing-mup-on-crime-and-disorder-public-safety-and-public-nuisance-report.pdf

47. Public Health Scotland. Monitoring and Evaluating Scotland's Alcohol Strategy (MESAS) monitoring report 2022; 2022. Available from: www.publichealthscotland.scot/media/13693/mesas-2022_english_jun2022.pdf

48. The Government's Alcohol Strategy. HM Government. London: HM Stationery Office; 2012. Available from: www.official-documents.gov.uk/document/cm83/8336/8336.aspthit

49. HM Government. Advancing our health: Prevention in the 2020s; 2019. Available from: https://assets.publishing.service.gov.uk/government/uploads/system/uploads/attachment_data/file/819766/advancing-our-health-prevention-in-the-2020s-accessible.pdf

50. Törrönen J, Roumeliotis F, Samuelsson E, Room R, Kraus L. How do social media-related attachments and assemblages encourage or reduce drinking among young people? Journal of Youth Studies. 2021;24(4):515–30.

Security without Obscurity

Obscurity

A Guide to PKI Operations

Security without Obscurity

Obscurity

A Guide to PKI Operations

J. J. Stapleton

W. Clay Epstein

CRC Press
Taylor & Francis Group
Boca Raton London New York

CRC Press is an imprint of the
Taylor & Francis Group, an **informa** business

AN AUERBACH BOOK

CRC Press
Taylor & Francis Group
6000 Broken Sound Parkway NW, Suite 300
Boca Raton, FL 33487-2742

First issued in paperback 2020

© 2016 by Taylor & Francis Group, LLC
CRC Press is an imprint of Taylor & Francis Group, an Informa business

No claim to original U.S. Government works

ISBN-13: 978-1-4987-0747-3 (hbk)
ISBN-13: 978-0-367-65864-9 (pbk)

Visit the Taylor & Francis Web site at
http://www.taylorandfrancis.com

and the CRC Press Web site at
http://www.crcpress.com

Contents

3

PREVALENCE OF RISKY ALCOHOL CONSUMPTION AMONGST ADULTS IN THE CRIMINAL JUSTICE

Introduction

As shown in previous chapters, alcohol harm and the harms related to it are a significant issue across the world. This is not only through the health and well-being consequences but also related to the link between alcohol consumption and crime and offending. As shown previously, an estimated 4% of worldwide deaths and 4–6% of global disability-adjusted life-years are linked to alcohol (1). Although the relationship is complex, there is an association between alcohol use and offending behaviour (2, 3), with an interplay between the amount drank, the pattern of drinking and individual and contextual factors (4).

Hazardous drinking is a repeated pattern of drinking that increases the risk of psychological or physical problems (5) whereas harmful drinking is defined by the presence of these problems (6). Drinking at hazardous or harmful levels is categorised as risky drinking.

By fully understanding the issue and the prevalence, we can explore how we tackle these issues. However, it has been shown that there is a complex interplay between individual and contextual factors and risky drinking behaviours and alcohol-related crime (7, 8). This chapter will explore alcohol use disorders and alcohol dependence prevalence of those involved across the different stages of the criminal justice system across the world.

The aim of this systematic review was to update and combine our previous reviews (9, 10) and to identify the levels of alcohol use disorders in the various stages of the criminal justice system around the world using validated prevalence tools. The evidence can be used to develop effective interventions in the criminal justice system.

We carried out a review of the international literature, using the Preferred Reporting Items for Systematic reviews and Meta-Analyses (PRISMA)

DOI: 10.4324/9781003169802-3

guidelines, which ensure comprehensive reporting within systematic reviews (11). This systematic review was conducted using the same methods to our previous reviews (9, 10). However, the original reviews only included prevalence in the UK using the AUDIT tool, whereas this review was extended to include worldwide literature using any validated tool.

Searches

The following databases, EBSCO (Child Development & Adolescent Studies, CINAHL Complete, Criminal Justice Abstracts with Full Text, MEDLINE, APA PsycArticles, Psychology and Behavioral Sciences Collection, APA PsycInfo) and Scopus, were searched using the search terms alcohol, screening, crime, police probation, court, jail, prison and variations of these in the title, keywords and abstract. Any language article was eligible for inclusion, but articles predating 2000 were not considered, and searches were restricted to 2000–present (January 2022). We only included articles where alcohol prevalence could be extracted.

Two authors were involved in the sifting of the published articles. One person reviewed all of them with another member of the team reviewing 20%. This was done in order to ascertain that all decisions matched, which they did, without the need for a third reviewer. Endnote was used to manage the data in the sifting stages, whilst data extraction was carried out using Microsoft Excel, which was again undertaken by two people. Data was extracted in the same way as our previous review, using the same data extraction tables, except that the country of study was added to the prevalence extraction table (9).

Grey literature was also searched from around the world, with variations of the search terms being entered into Google and the first 300 hits were investigated by Natalie Connor, Andrew Divers and Gillian Waller. We also interrogated our previous articles on the subject (9, 12), screened the reference lists of included articles and reached out through the International Network on Brief Interventions for Alcohol & Other Drugs (INEBRIA – http://inebria.net/) and Twitter to obtain any further articles, and to ensure no potentially relevant studies had been overlooked.

This systematic review sought to identify the prevalence of alcohol use disorders in the criminal justice system worldwide by searching the available evidence. To ensure reliability, it was important for articles to use a screening tool that is validated when assessing the prevalence of alcohol use disorders (9). We included articles that used a validated prevalence tool. These included the AUDIT, MAST, CAGE and WHO ASSIST.

AUDIT

The Alcohol Use Disorders Identification Test (AUDIT) is considered to be the gold standard of tools used to identify alcohol use disorders in healthcare settings (13). The ten-question AUDIT is scored between 0 and 40. A score of 8+ for adults indicates an alcohol use disorder; 8–15 indicates hazardous drinking, 16–19 harmful drinking and a score of 20+ indicates probable dependence (5). It has been shown to have 92% sensitivity and 94% specificity (5). Furthermore, it has been shown to be effective in the various stages of the criminal justice system (14).

MAST

Reliability and validity studies indicate that the Michigan Alcoholism Screening Test (MAST) can be used for identification of alcohol-related problems in a variety of settings, with sensitivity rates ranging from 0.75 to 0.90 (15). Scores range from 0 to 53. The scoring system is very sensitive at the five-point level, with a score of 5 placing a respondent in the hazardous drinking range (16).

CAGE

The four item Cut, Annoyed, Guilty, Eye-opener (CAGE) questionnaire can be used to detect alcohol-related issues. The CAGE scale, when used with one or more yes responses indicating a positive response, achieved a sensitivity of 86% and specificity of 93% when using the diagnostic interview as the criterion standard (17).

World Health Organization – ASSIST

The ASSIST is an instrument developed by the World Health Organization to screen for hazardous, harmful and dependent use of tobacco, alcohol and drugs (nonmedical use). The ASSIST has high internal consistency across drugs examined (0.77–0.94) and acceptable correlations between ASSIST scores and measures of risk factors for alcohol and drug use problems (0.48–0.76) (18). Following ASSIST administration, separate risk scores for each drug are calculated, with scores falling within a low-, moderate-, or high-risk range (18).

Quality assessment

The relevant screening tools from the Critical Appraisal Skills Programme (CASP) were used to quality assess any included articles within this review (19). The quality assessment was carried out by one person and 20% checked by another. High risk of bias was recorded if 'no' or 'unsure' was recorded for 6 or more of the 11 questions on the tool. Medium risk of bias was assigned if 'no' or 'unsure' was recorded for 4–5 questions and low risk for 1–3 questions, as in our previous study (12).

Results

In total 10,898 articles were identified from the initial searches. Following the first sift, 189 full articles were assessed for inclusion. After the completion of the full text screening, 41 articles were deemed eligible for inclusion (Tables 3.1–3.4). Figure 3.1 provides a breakdown of the numbers of articles and grey literature excluded at each stage.

The majority of articles (*n* = 25) were from the UK (4, 14, 20–42), four from the USA (43–46), three from France (47–49) and two each from Australia (50, 51) and Sweden (52, 53) and one each from Brazil (54), Ethiopia (55), Holland (56), Norway (57) and Ukraine (58). The majority of participants were males (80%).

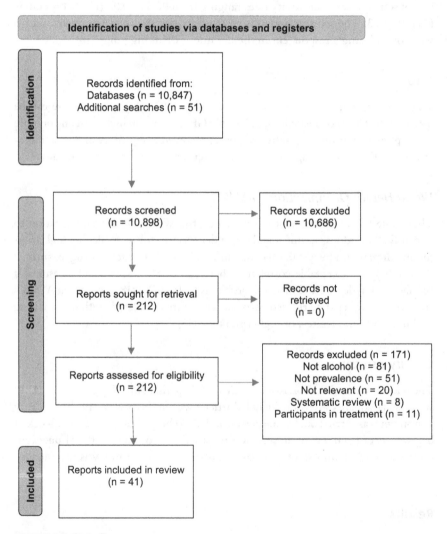

FIGURE 3.1 Data flow

TABLE 3.1 Prevalence rates – other settings

Author (year)	Country	% m/f (total n)	Age	Tool used	Alcohol use disorder positive	Alcohol use disorder ranges
Magistrates court						
Watt et al. (29)	Wales	100% male (n = 262)	I: 23.6 ± 4.7 C: 22.8 ± 4.6	AUDIT	95%	PD = 39%
Police, probation and prison together						
Coulton et al. (14)	England	57% male (n = 205)	31.1 ± 9.9	AUDIT	73%	Haz = 26%; harm/ DP = 75%

Notes: M, male; F, female; Haz, hazardous drinking; Harm, harmful drinking; PD, probably dependent.

Police, probation and prison together

One study of low risk from England included participants from the police, probation and prison together (14) (Table 3.1). The study used the AUDIT screening tool, needed included 205 participants and showed that 73% had an alcohol use disorder (8+ on AUDIT) with 26% as hazardous drinkers and 75% harmful or possibly dependent (20+ on AUDIT).

Magistrates' court

One study was found (low risk) in relation to prevalence amongst those at a magistrates' court in Wales (29) (Table 3.1). Of those screened 95% scored positive for an alcohol use disorder (8+ on AUDIT) and 39% as being probably dependent (20+ on AUDIT). The eligibility for the study, however, was that the participant had been sentenced for a violent crime committed whilst intoxicated. This would explain the high prevalence rates however did not include 100% of those that took part (Table 3.1).

Police custody suites

Nine studies were found relating to the police custody suite setting (20–22, 24–28, 52): six studies were classified as low risk (20, 22, 24, 27, 52), two as medium risk (25, 26) and one as high risk (28) (Table 3.2). Eight were conducted in England and one in Sweden (52) and included 12,897 participants (range 12–4,739) and the majority of participants were male (Table 3.2).

Two of the studies gave mean AUDIT scores 14.7 + 10.19 and 14.66 + 10.19 (28, 52). The prevalence of AUDIT positives (8+) ranged from 26% to 88% with the

TABLE 3.2 Prevalence rates – police custody suites

Author (year)	Country	% m/f (total n)	Age	Tool used	Alcohol use disorder positive	Alcohol use disorder ranges
Addison et al. (20)	England	Not given (n = 720)	18+	AUDIT	54%	None given
Barton (21)	England	85% male (n = 3,900)	17+	AUDIT	64%	Haz = 32%; Harm = 11%; PD = 21%
Brown et al. (22)	England	81% male (n = 229)	29.4 + 11	AUDIT	76%	None given
Durbeej et al. (52)	Sweden	91% male (n = 181)	33 + 10.9	AUDIT	14.66 + 10.19	None given
Hopkins & Sparrow (24)	England	89% male (n = 805)	Mean = 27	AUDIT	88%	PD = 35%
Kennedy et al. (25)	England	83% male (n = 2,177)	18+	AUDIT	84%	Haz = 38%; Harm = 11%; PD = 38%
McCracken et al. (26)	England	86% male (n = 4,739)	18+	AUDIT	85%	Haz = 36%; Harm = 13%; PD = 37%
Samele et al. (27)	England	93% male (n = 134)	31.2 + 10.4	AUDIT	26%	None given
Tobutt & Milani (28)	England	92% male (n = 12)	18+	AUDIT	14.9 ± 1.4	None given

Notes: M, male; F, female; Haz, hazardous drinking; Harm, harmful drinking; PD, probably dependent.

median being 76%. Four studies reported prevalence of probable dependence (20+) (21, 24–26). These ranged from 21% to 38% (Table 3.2).

Probation

Ten studies from nine articles were found in the probation setting (23, 30, 32–34, 38, 43, 56, 59): six were classified as low risk (33, 34, 38, 43, 56, 59), two medium risk (30, 32) and one high risk (23). Eight were conducted in the UK (23, 30, 32–34, 38, 59), one in Holland (56) and one in the USA (43). The studies included 2,667 participants (range 32–525) with the majority of participants being male. Two studies gave mean AUDIT scores 11.6 ± 10.7 and 7.2 ± 8.5 (38, 56). Prevalence rates for an alcohol use disorder (8+) ranged from 31% to 87.5% and probable dependence (20+) between 5% and 36%. Two studies gave prevalence rates for women; AUDIT positive 20% and 53%, probable dependence was 25% and 5% (34, 56) (Table 3.3).

Prison

The majority of studies were found in the prison system. We found 23 studies from 22 articles (4, 31, 34, 36, 37, 39–42, 44–51, 53–55, 57, 58). Thirteen studies were classified as low risk (4, 34, 39, 41, 44, 47, 49, 51, 53–55, 57, 58) and the rest as medium risk (31, 36, 37, 40, 42, 46, 48, 50). Nine were conducted in the UK (4, 31, 34, 36, 37, 39–42), three in France (47–49) and the USA (44–46), two in Australia (50, 51) and one in Ukraine (58), Sweden (53), Brazil (54), Norway (57) and Ethiopia (55). The studies included 8,570 participants (range 47–1,446).

Prevalence rates ranged from 11% to 86% for an alcohol use disorder. This differed across different tools used.

AUDIT

Fifteen articles used the AUDIT tool (4, 29, 31, 34, 36, 37, 40, 41, 47, 51, 53–55, 57, 58). Rates of alcohol use disorder ranged from 19% to 82%. Probable dependence ranged from 21% to 49% (Table 3.4).

CAGE

Three articles used the CAGE (46, 48, 49). The prevalence of alcohol use disorders was 14% (49), 17% (48) and 46% (46) (Table 3.4).

MAST

Two articles used the MAST (42, 45). One study showed an alcohol use disorder rate of 54% (42) and the other showed an alcohol use disorder rate of 61% (45) (Table 3.4).

TABLE 3.3 Prevalence rates – probation

Author (year)	Country	% m/f (total n)	Age	Tool used	Alcohol use disorder positive	Alcohol use disorder ranges
Dong et al. (43)	USA	72% male (n = 304)	Med 36	AUDIT	87.5%	Haz = 24%; Harm 41%; PD = 22%
Fitton et al. (23)	England	100% male (n = 32)	58.1 + 6.9	AUDIT	31%	Mean AUDIT 7.2 + 8.5
Hildebrand & Noteborn (56)	Holland	86% male (n = 371)	Not given	AUDIT	M = 47% F = 20%	M-PD = 12%; F-PD = 5%
Lader et al. (30)	England & Wales	Remand: 92% male (n = 339)	16+	AUDIT	M = 62%; F = 13%	M-Haz = 28%; M-Harm/PD = 33%. F-Haz = 5%; M-Harm/PD = 8%
Lader et al. (30)	England & Wales	Sentenced: 68% male (n = 250)	16+	AUDIT	M = 70%; F = 51%	M-Haz = 34%; M-Harm/PD = 36%. F-Haz 25%; M-Harm/PD = 25%
MacAskill et al. (59)	Scotland	100% male (n = 216)	18-64	AUDIT	73%	Haz 27%; Harm = 9%; PD = 36%
Newbury-Birch et al. (34)	England	86% male (n = 262)	18+	AUDIT	M = 69% F = 53%	M-Haz = 26%; M-Harm n = 11%; M-PD = 35%. F-Haz = 25%; F-Harm = 3%; F-PD = 25%
Newbury-Birch et al. (33)	England	85% male (n = 525)	31 + 10.9	AUDIT	86%	Haz = 43%; Harm/Dep = 42%
Orr et al. (32)	Scotland	85% male (n = 195)	Mean = 31	AUDIT	59%	PD = 17%
Pluck et al. (38)	England	87% male (n = 173)	36.0 ± 13.5	AUDIT	11.6 ± 10.7	PD = 23%

Notes: M, male; F, female; Haz, hazardous drinking; Harm, harmful drinking; PD, probably dependent.

ASSIST

Two articles used the ASSIST (44, 50). One study showed an alcohol use disorder rate of 20% for males and 11% for females (50) and the other showed an alcohol use disorder rate of 43% (44) (Table 3.4).

In relation to quality assessment, we found that the majority ($n = 26$) of the included studies had a low risk of bias (4, 14, 20–22, 24, 27, 29, 33, 34, 38, 39, 41, 43, 44, 47, 49, 51–59), 12 had a medium risk (25, 26, 30–32, 36, 37, 40, 42, 46, 48, 50) and three a high risk of bias (23, 28, 45) (Table 3.5).

Discussion

We carried out a systematic review of the international literature to ascertain levels of alcohol use disorders and included 41 studies within the analysis. This gives us an overview of alcohol use disorders and probable dependence across the world.

As expected we found high levels of alcohol use disorders in all stages of the criminal justice system with levels as high as 86% compared to around 24% in the general population in England (60). We also found very high levels of alcohol dependence across the different stages of the criminal justice system with levels as high as 49% compared to around 1.4% in the general population in the UK (61). This disparity in prevalence rates help us understand what interventions are needed in the criminal justice system.

One of the main issues when looking at alcohol use disorders in any setting is how we measure it using validated tools so we can compare across different parts of the criminal justice system. It has long been shown that working with those in the criminal justice system can be challenging, in large due to the population being 'hard to reach' and often falling victim to their chaotic lifestyles (32).

One of the fundamental issues is that studies include different measurement tools and outcomes, with outcomes decided upon based on the research funding.

The INEBRIA convened a Research Measurement Standardization Special Interest Group to establish a Core Outcome Set for Alcohol Brief Interventions (ABIs) in 2014. The group used the Core Outcome Measures in Effectiveness Trials (COMET) guidelines for Core Outcome Measures development (62). The work comprised of three phases: a systematic review, outcomes summarised and then an e-Delphi exercise based on the previous phase (63–65).

Ten outcomes and recommended measures were selected for screening and for future trials of alcohol screening and brief interventions (Table 3.6) (63–65). These should be carried out using validated and reliable places.

However, in research studies in the criminal justice system, we also need to include outcomes that are relevant to recidivism, whether that is data relating to arrest, charge, conviction or time to reconviction and this needs to be examined further; however, to date, there is a lack of studies to enable us to give this information (10).

TABLE 3.4 Prevalence rates – prison

Author (year)	Country	% m/f (total n)	Age	Tool used	Alcohol use disorder positive	Alcohol use disorder ranges
Azbel et al. (58)	Ukraine	80% male (n = 402)	31.9	AUDIT	57%	None given
Begun et al. (36)	England	100% female (n = 1,181)	18+	AUDIT	67%	None given
Graham et al. (4)	Scotland	100% male (n = 96)	18+	AUDIT	73%	Haz = 25%; Harm = 43%; PD = 43%
Haile et al. (55)	Ethiopia	100% male (n = 347)	27.8 + 11.4	AUDIT	59%	PD = 21%
Hassan et al. (42)	England & Wales	69% male (n = 409)	33.0 + 8.7	MAST	54%	None given
Holloway et al. (41)	England & Scotland	100% male (n = 502)	33 + 10	AUDIT	80% sentenced; 82% remand	PD 34% sentenced & 49% remand
Holmwood et al. (50)	Australia	86% male (n = 518)	Not given	ASSIST	M = 20%; F = 11%	M-Mod = 15%; M-High = 5%; F-Mod = 8%; F-High = 3%
Kerslake et al. (51)	Australia	91% male (n = 371)	34.1 + 9.3	AUDIT	35%	None given
Kissell et al. (40)	England	100% male (n = 242)	26.5	AUDIT	81%	PD = 48%
Konstenius et al. (53)	Sweden	100% female (n = 96)	39.7	AUDIT	33%	21% 6–17 on AUDIT; 22% > 18 on AUDIT
Maggia et al. (47)	France	100% male (n = 47)	27.3 + 8	AUDIT	19%	None given
McMurran & Cusens (31)	England	100% male (n = 126)	30.52 + 10	AUDIT	86%	None given
Michaud et al. (48)	France	100% male (n = 191)	Not given	CAGE	17%	None given
Newbury-Birch et al. (34)	England	94% male (n = 411)	18+	AUDIT	M = 59%; F = 63%	M-Haz = 19%; M-Harm = 4%; M-PD = 36%. F-Haz = 21%; F-Harm = 0; F-PD = 42%

Nunes et al. (54)	Brazil	100% female (n = 178)	34.2 + 9.6	AUDIT	7.25 + 10.6	None given
Pape et al. (57)	Norway	94% male (n = 1,446)	Not given	AUDIT	55%	PD = 18%
Parkes et al. (37)	Scotland	Remand: 100% male (n = 137)	Median = 27	AUDIT	68%	Haz = 24%; Harm = 10%; PD = 34%
Parkes et al. (37)	Scotland	Sentenced: 100% male (n = 122)	Median = 27	AUDIT	83%	Haz = 31%; Harm = 9%; PD = 39%
Prendergast et al. (44)	USA	73% male (n = 732)	37.6 + 11.4	ASSIST	43%	Medium = 25%; High = 18%
Sahajian et al. (49)	France	100% female (n = 534)	31.5 + 13.7	CAGE	14%	None given
Wainwright et al. (39)	England & Wales	100% male (n = 105)	42 + 14	AUDIT	56%	Mean 13.87 + 12.10
White et al. (45)	USA	100% male (n = 115)	19–29 = 36%; 30–39 = 29%; 40+ = 36%	MAST	61%	None given
Williams et al. (46)	USA	94% male (n = 360)	61 (55–84)	CAGE	46%	None given

Notes: M, male; F, female; Haz, hazardous drinking; Harm, harmful drinking; PD, probably dependent.

TABLE 3.5 Quality assessment/risk of bias

Author (year)	Quality assessment
Police custody suites	
Addison et al. (20)	Low risk
Barton (21)	Low risk
Brown et al. (22)	Low risk
Durbeej et al. (52)	Low risk
Hopkins & Sparrow (24)	Low risk
Kennedy et al. (25)	Medium risk
Mccracken et al. (26)	Medium risk
Samele et al. (27)	Low risk
Tobutt & Milani (28)	High risk
Magistrates court	
Watt et al. (29)	Low risk
Probation	
Lader et al. (30)	Medium risk
Newbury-Birch et al. (34)*	Low risk
MacAskill et al. (59)	Low risk
Newbury-Birch et al. (33)	Low risk
Pluck et al. (38)	Low risk
Orr et al. (32)	Medium risk
Hildebrand & Noteborn (56)	Low risk
Dong et al. (43)	Low risk
Fitton et al. (23)	High risk
Prison	
Michaud et al. (48)	Medium risk
White et al. (45)	High risk
Maggia et al. (47)	Low risk
McMurran & Cusens (31)	Medium risk
Holmwood et al. (50)	Medium risk
Sahajin et al. (49)	Low risk
Newbury-Birch et al. (34)*	Low risk
Williams et al. (46)	Medium risk
Begun et al. (36)	Medium risk
Parkes et al. (37)	Medium risk
Graham et al. (4)	Low risk
Hassan et al. (42)	Medium risk
Konstenius et al. (53)	Low risk
Azbel et al. (58)	Low risk
Nunes et al. (54)	Low risk
Kissell et al. (40)	Medium risk
Prendergast et al. (44)	Low risk
Wainwright et al. (39)	Low risk
Holloway et al. (41)	Low risk
Haile et al. (55)	Low risk
Kerslake et al. (51)	Low risk
Pape et al. (57)	Low risk
Police, probation and prison together	
Coulton et al. (14)	Low risk

* Indicates the same study but different populations.

TABLE 3.6 Core outcome set for alcohol screening and brief intervention studies

Outcome 1	Typical frequency of consumption
Outcome 2	Typical quantity of consumption
Outcome 3	Frequency of heavy episodic drinking
Outcome 4	Combined consumption measure
Outcome 5	Hazardous or harmful drinking
Outcome 6	Standard drinks consumed in the past week
Outcome 7	Alcohol-related consequences
Outcome 8	Alcohol-related injury
Outcome 9	Use of emergency healthcare services
Outcome 10	Quality of life

Chapter summary

This systematic review shows that levels of alcohol use disorders and probable dependence are far higher across all stages of the criminal justice system than they are in healthcare settings. Forty-one articles were included in the analysis. We included articles from the UK, USA, France, Australia, Sweden, Brazil, Ethiopia, Holland, Norway and Ukraine. We found high levels of alcohol use disorders in all areas of the criminal justice system, for example, 21–38% in the police custody setting, 31–87.5% in the probation setting and 11–86% in the prison setting. More work is needed to fully explore how these findings relate to intervention development. There is a need for more robust studies that use the same outcome tools for measuring alcohol use disorders and dependence. This information is imperative to designing interventions across the criminal justice system.

References

1. Rehm J, Mathers C, Popova S, Thavorncharoensap M, Teerawattananon Y, Patra J. Global burden of disease and injury and economic cost attributable to alcohol use and alcohol-use disorders. Lancet. 2009;373:2223–33.
2. Boden J, Fergusson D, Horwood L. Alcohol misuse and violent behavior: Findings from a 30-year longitudinal study. Drug & Alcohol Dependence. 2012;122(1–2):135–41.
3. Richardson A, Budd T. Alcohol, crime and disorder: A study of young adults. February. Report No.: Home Office Research Study 263. London: Home Office Research, Development and Statistics Directorate; 2003
4. Graham L, Heller-Murphy S, Aitken L, McAuley A. Alcohol problems in a remand Scottish prisoner population. International Journal of Prisoner Health. 2012;8(2):51–9.
5. Saunders JB, Aasland OG, Babor TF, De La Fuente JR, Grant M. Development of the Alcohol Use Disorders Identification Test (AUDIT): WHO collaborative project on early detection of persons with harmful alcohol consumption. Addiction. 1993;88(6):791–804.
6. World Health Organization. The role of general practice settings in the prevention and management of the harm done by alcohol. Copenhagen: World Health Organization Regional Office for Europe; 1992.

7. Graham L, Parkes T, McAuley A, Doi L. Alcohol problems in the criminal justice system: An opportunity for intervention. Denmark: World Health Organization Regional Office for Europe; 2012.

8. Lightowlers C, Elliot M, Tranmer M. The dynamic risk of heavy episodic drinking on interpersonal assault in young adolescence and early adulthood. British Journal of Criminology. 2014;54(6):1207–27.

9. Newbury-Birch D, McGovern R, Birch J, O'Neill G, Kaner H, Sondhi A, et al. A rapid systematic review of what we know about alcohol use disorders and brief interventions in the criminal justice system. International Journal of Prisoner Health. 2016;12(1):57–70.

10. Newbury-Birch D, Ferguson J, Connor N, Divers A, Waller G. A rapid systematic review of worldwide alcohol use disorders and brief alcohol interventions in the criminal justice system. Frontiers in Psychiatry-Addictive Disorders. 2022;13:900186. doi: 10.3389/fpsyt.2022.900186

11. Rethlefsen ML, Kirtley S, Waffenschmidt S, Ayala AP, Moher D, Page MJ, et al. PRISMA-S: An extension to the PRISMA statement for reporting literature searches in systematic reviews. Systematic Reviews. 2021;10(1):39.

12. Newbury-Birch D, Ferguson J, Landale S, Giles EL, McGeechan GJ, Gill C, et al. A systematic review of the efficacy of alcohol interventions for incarcerated people. Alcohol and Alcoholism. 2018;53(4):412–25.

13. Hodgson R, Alwyn T, John B, Thom B, Smith A. The FAST alcohol screening test. Alcohol and Alcoholism. 2002;37(1):61–6.

14. Coulton S, Newbury-Birch D, Cassidy P, Dale V, Deluca P, Gilvarry E, et al. Screening for alcohol use in criminal justice settings: An exploratory study. Alcohol and Alcoholism. 2012;47(4):423–7.

15. Storgaard H, Nielsen S, Gluud C. The validity of the Michigan Alcohol Screening Test (MAST). Alcohol and Alcoholism. 1994;29:493–502.

16. Selzer ML. The Michigan Alcoholism Screening Test (MAST): The quest for a new diagnostic instrument. American Journal of Psychiatry. 1971;127:1653–8.

17. Liskow B, Campbell J, Nickel EJ, Powell BJ. Validity of the CAGE questionnaire in screening for alcohol dependence in a walk-in (triage) clinic. Journal of Studies on Alcohol and Drugs. 1995;56(3):277–81.

18. Humeniuk R, Ali R, Babor TF, Farrell M, Formigoni ML, Jittiwutikarn J, et al. Validation of the alcohol, smoking and substance involvement screening test (ASSIST). Addiction. 2008;103(6):1039–47.

19. CASP-UK. Critical appraisal skills programme (CASP). London, Oxford; 2002. https://casp-uk.net

20. Addison M, McGovern R, Angus C, Becker F, Brennan A, Brown H, et al. Alcohol screening and brief intervention in police custody suites: Pilot Cluster Randomised Controlled Trial (AcCePT). Alcohol and Alcoholism. 2018;53(5):548–59.

21. Barton A. Screening and brief intervention of detainees for alcohol use: A social crime prevention approach to combating alcohol-related crime? The Howard Journal. 2011;50(1):62–74.

22. Brown N, Newbury-Birch D, McGovern R, Phinn E, Kaner E. Alcohol screening and brief intervention in a policing context: A mixed methods feasibility study. Drug & Alcohol Review. 2010;29:647–54.

23. Fitton L, Bates A, Hayes A, Fazel S. Psychiatric disorders, substance use, and executive functioning in older probationers. Criminal Behaviour and Mental Health. 2018;28(6):447–59.

24. Hopkins M, Sparrow P. Sobering up: Arrest referral and brief intervention for alcohol users in the custody suite. Criminology and Criminal Justice. 2006;6(4):389–410.

25. Kennedy A, Dunbar I, Boath M, Beynon C, Duffy P, Stafford J, et al. Evaluation of alcohol arrest referral Pilot Schemes (Phase 1). London: Home Office; 2012.

26. McCracken K, McMurran M, Winlow S, Sassi F, McCarthy K. Evaluation of alcohol arrest referral pilot schemes (Phase 2) . London: Home Office; 2012. Available from: www.gov.uk/government/uploads/system/uploads/attachment_data/file/116 267/occ102.pdf

27. Samele C, McKinnon I, Brown P, Srivastava S, Arnold A, Hallett N, et al. The prevalence of mental illness and unmet needs of police custody detainees. Criminal Behaviour and Mental Health. 2021;31(2):80–95.

28. Tobutt C, Milani R. Comparing two counselling styles for hazardous drinkers charged with alcohol-related offences in a police custody suite: Piloting motivational interviewing brief intervention or a standard brief intervention to reduce alcohol consumption. Advances in Dual Diagnosis. 2010;3(4):20–33.

29. Watt K, Shepherd J, Newcombe R. Drunk and dangerous: A randomised controlled trial of alcohol brief intervention for violent offenders. Journal of Experimental Criminology. 2008;4(1):1–19.

30. Lader D, Singleton N, Meltzer H. Psychiatric morbidity among young offenders in England and Wales. London: Office for National Statistics; 2000.

31. McMurran M, Cusens B. Alcohol and violent and non-violent acquisitive offending. Addiction Research and Theory. 2005;13(5):439–43.

32. Orr K, McCoard S, Canning S, McCartney P, Williams J. Delivery alcohol brief interventions in the community justice setting: Evaluation of a pilot project. Glasgow: NHS Health Scotland; 2011.

33. Newbury-Birch D, Coulton S, Bland M, Cassidy P, Dale V, Deluca P, et al. Alcohol screening and brief interventions for offenders in the probation setting (SIPS Trial): A pragmatic multicentre cluster randomised controlled trial. Alcohol and Alcoholism. 2014;49(5):540–8.

34. Newbury-Birch D, Harrison B, Brown N, Kaner E. Sloshed and sentenced: A prevalence study of alcohol use disorders among offenders in the North East of England. International Journal of Prisoner Health. 2009;5(4):201–11.

35. Newbury-Birch D, Jackson K, Hodgson T, Gilvarry E, Cassidy P, Coulton S, et al. Alcohol-related risk and harm amongst young offenders aged 11–17. International Journal of Prisoner Health. 2015;11(2):75–86.

36. Begun A, Rose L, LeBel T. Intervening with women in jail around alcohol and substance abuse during preparation for community reentry. Alcoholism Treatment Quarterly. 2011;29(4):453–78.

37. Parkes T, MacAskill S, Brooks O, Jepson R, Atherton I, Doi L, et al. Prison health needs assessment for alcohol problems. Edinburgh: NHS Health Scotland; 2011.

38. Pluck G, Brooker C, Blizard R, Moran P. Personality disorder in a probation cohort: Demographic, substance misuse and forensic characteristics. Criminal Behaviour and Mental Health. 2015;25(5):403–15.

39. Wainwright V, Lennox C, McDonnell S, Shaw J, Senior J. The mental health and substance misuse needs of male ex-armed forces personnel in prison. Journal of Forensic Psychiatry and Psychology. 2018;29(1):146–62.

40. Kissell A, Taylor P, Walker J, Lewis E, Hammond A, Amos T. Disentangling alcohol-related needs among pre-trial prisoners: A longitudinal study. Alcohol and Alcoholism. 2014;49(6):639–44.

41. Holloway A, Ferguson J, Parker R, Sheik A, Guthrie V, Newbury-Birch D. Alcohol brief interventions for male remand prisoners: A mixed-methods feasibility and acceptability study. Lancet. 2019;394:S53.
42. Hassan L, Rahman M, King C, Senior J, Shaw J. Level of mental health intervention and clinical need among inmates with mental illness in five English jails. Psychiatric Services. 2012;63(12):1218–24.
43. Dong KR, Must A, Tang AM, Stopka TJ, Beckwith CG. Food insecurity, morbidities, and substance use in adults on probation in Rhode Island. Journal of Urban Health. 2018;95(4):564–75.
44. Prendergast ML, McCollister K, Warda U. A randomized study of the use of screening, brief intervention, and referral to treatment (SBIRT) for drug and alcohol use with jail inmates. Journal of Substance Abuse Treatment. 2017;74:54–64.
45. White RJ, Ackerman RJ, Caraveo LE. Self-identified alcohol abusers in a low-security federal prison: Characteristics and treatment implications. International Journal of Offender Therapy and Comparative Criminology. 2001;45(2):214–27.
46. Williams B, McGuire J, LIndsay R, Baillargeon J, Lee S, Kushel M. Coming home: Health status and homelessness risk of older pre-release prisoners. Journal of General Internal Medicine. 2010;25(10):1038–44.
47. Maggia B, Martin S, Crouzet C, Richard P, Wagner P, Balmès J-L, et al. Variation in AUDIT (Alcohol Use [correction of Used] Disorder Identification Test) scores within the first weeks of imprisonment. Alcohol and Alcoholism (Oxford, Oxfordshire). 2004;39(3):247–50.
48. Michaud Ph, Pessione F, Lavault J, Rohmer G, Rueff B. Screening of alcohol-related problems in French detainees using the cage questionnaire. Alcologia. 2000;12(1):19–25.
49. Sahajian F, Lamothe P, Fabry J, Vanhems P. Consumption of psychoactive substances among 535 women entering a Lyon prison (France) between June 2004 and December 2008. Revue d'Epidemiologie et de Sante Publique. 2012;60(5):371–81.
50. Holmwood C, Marriott M, Humeniuk R. Substance use patterns in newly admitted male and female South Australian prisoners using the WHO-ASSIST (Alcohol, Smoking and Substance Involvement Screening Test). International Journal of Prisoner Health. 2008;4(4):198–207.
51. Kerslake M, Simpson M, Richmond R, Albany H, Butler T. Risky alcohol consumption prior to incarceration: A cross-sectional study of drinking patterns among Australian prison entrants. Drug & Alcohol Review. 2020;39(6):694–703.
52. Durbeej N, Berman AH, Gumpert CH, Palmstierna T, Kristiansson M, Alm C. Validation of the alcohol use disorders identification test and the drug use disorders identification test in a Swedish sample of suspected offenders with signs of mental health problems: Results from the Mental Disorder, Substance Abuse and Crime study. Journal of Substance Abuse Treatment. 2010;39(4):364–77.
53. Konstenius M, Larsson H, Lundholm L, Philips B, van de Glind G, Jayaram-Lindström N, et al. An epidemiological study of ADHD, substance use, and comorbid problems in incarcerated women in Sweden. Journal of Attention Disorders. 2012;19(1):44–52.
54. Nunes AdM, Baltieri DA. Substance misuse subtypes among women convicted of homicide. Substance Abuse. 2013;34(2):169–78.
55. Haile YG, Kebede KB, Limenhe A, Habatmu K, Alem A. Alcohol use disorder among prisoners in Debre Berhan prison, Ethiopia: A cross-sectional study.

Substance Abuse: Treatment, Prevention, and Policy. 2020;15(1):26. https://doi.org/10.1186/s13011-020-00270-w

56. Hildebrand M, Noteborn MGC. Exploration of the (interrater) reliability and latent factor structure of the alcohol use disorders identification test (AUDIT) and the drug use disorders identification test (DUDIT) in a sample of Dutch probationers. Substance Use and Misuse. 2015;50(10):1294–306.

57. Pape H, Rossow I, Bukten A. Alcohol problems among prisoners: Subgroup variations, concurrent drug problems, and treatment needs. European Addiction Research. 2021;27(3):179–88.

58. Azbel L, Wickersham J, Grishaev Y, Dvoryak S, Altice F. Burden of infectious diseases, substance use disorders, and mental illness among Ukrainian prisoners transitioning to the community. PLoS One. 2013;8(3):e59643.

59. MacAskill S, Parkes T, Brooks O, Graham L, McAuley A, Brown A. Assessment of alcohol problems using AUDIT in a prison setting: More than an 'aye or no' question. BMC Public Health. 2011;11:865.

60. Burton R, Henn C, Lavoie D, O'Connor R, Perkins C, Sweeney C, et al. The public health burden of alcohol: Evidence review. London: Public Health England.; 2016.

61. Public Health England. Alcohol dependence prevalence in England. London: Public Health England; 2021.

62. Williamson P, Clarke M. The COMET (Core Outcome Measures in Effectiveness Trials) Initiative: Its role in improving Cochrane reviews. Cochrane Database of Systematic Reviews. 2012; ED000041.

63. Shorter G, Heather N, Bray J, Giles E, Holloway A, Barbosa C, et al. The 'Outcome Reporting in Brief Intervention Trials: Alcohol' (ORBITAL) framework: Protocol to determine a core outcome set for efficacy and effectiveness trials of alcohol screening and brief intervention. Trials. 2018;18(1):611.

64. Shorter GW, Bray JW, Giles EL, O'donnell AJ, Berman AH, Holloway A, et al. The variability of outcomes used in efficacy and effectiveness trials of alcohol brief interventions: A systematic review. Journal of Studies on Alcohol and Drugs. 2019;80(3):286–98.

65. Shorter GW, Heather N, Bray JW, Berman AH, Giles EL, O'Donnell AJ, et al. Prioritization of outcomes in efficacy and effectiveness of alcohol brief intervention trials: International multi-stakeholder e-delphi consensus study to inform a core outcome set. Journal of Studies on Alcohol and Drugs. 2019;80(3):299–309.

4

RISKY DRINKING AMONGST MEN IN THE CRIMINAL JUSTICE SYSTEM

Introduction

This chapter will start with a discussion of the prevalence of risky drinking amongst men in the criminal justice system and explore that prevalence with reference to current research studies and relevant demographics and inequalities suffered by men who are involved in the criminal justice system. In the UK, between 51 and 83% of incarcerated people are classified as risky drinkers (1) and for those on remand in prison, the prevalence is between 62 and 68% (2). Furthermore, alcohol dependence among those incarcerated (43%) is ten times higher than the general population (2). There are significantly more men in prison than their female counterparts meaning male prisons make up 96% of the entire population (3). Screening and alcohol brief interventions can be a cost-effective way to help reduce the alcohol use of a captive audience if delivering them within the criminal justice system. This chapter discusses this in depth, specifically in relation to the male prison population.

Men and alcohol

Prevalence of risky drinking and men

As discussed throughout earlier chapters, those individuals who misuse alcohol and drink at a risky level are said to have an alcohol use disorder (4). Within the general population in the UK, there are around 26% of adults with an alcohol use disorder (38% of men, 16% of women aged 16–64) (5). Furthermore, 3.6% of the general population in the UK are estimated to be dependent on alcohol (6% of men and 2% of women) (6).

The World Health Organization (WHO) has stated 'worldwide, heavy alcohol consumption is a leading cause of ill health and premature death' (7). In addition

DOI: 10.4324/9781003169802-4

to the often-discussed health effects, there are many negative social consequences of alcohol use to consider. Risky drinking can lead to sexual risk-taking, being involved in crime, personal injuries and many types of violence (8). There are also many other social consequences such as problems at work, traffic problems, neglecting major obligations and problems with partners (9). There is a wide range of these negative social consequences that can lead to many individuals becoming involved in the criminal justice system and even incarcerated and therefore should feature prominently in any intervention delivered to this population.

Data from the Crime Survey for England and Wales show that in almost half of all violent crimes, the victim perceived the offender to be under the influence of alcohol (10). A recent review by the authors found that up to 86% of men and 63% of women in the UK criminal justice system scored positive for an alcohol use disorder (11). This compares to just 24% of the general population in the UK (12, 13). Tyler et al. found that men in prison were significantly more likely than women to screen positive for problematic alcohol use and have used drugs prior to entering prison (14). Thus, demonstrating a need to consider alcohol interventions tailored towards those in the criminal justice system. For reasons detailed later in Chapter 5, it is essential to consider a gendered approach when working with this population of individuals.

Men in the criminal justice system

The criminal justice system refers to 'those institutions that respond to the commission of offences' (15) including the prison setting, both open and closed, police custody setting, youth offending services and probation.

Throughout the various stages of the criminal justice system, from arrest to incarceration in prison to probation, the prevalence of men moving through the system is higher. This starts even with stop and search. According to the UK Home Office (16) statistics, 66% of stop and searches carried out between April 2021 and March 2022 were of men aged between 15 and 34. Furthermore, this data showed that the rates of stop and search varied depending upon ethnicity and location (16). Similarly with arrests of males, approximately 85% of arrests are of men, accounting for 561,211 arrests made in 2021/22 (16). Of those arrests, 44% were in relation to violence against the person offences, the most common type of offence followed by theft (12%). As of June 2022, there were just over 220,000 men supervised by probation services in England and Wales (17).

Males in the criminal justice system, like their female counterparts, suffer from a range of inequalities within society. This is relevant to both men and boys. Despite only 1% of children in England being looked after, 33% of boys in custody are in care (1). In addition, 7.3% of looked after children encounter the youth justice system, in comparison to 3% of all children (2).

The Lammy Review (18) documented the ways in which individuals from minority ethnic backgrounds are overrepresented within the criminal justice system. The review found disproportionate percentages of black, Asian and minority ethnic (BAME) people with relation to arrest rates, stop and searches, and custodial sentences (18). For example, 25% of the adult prison population are BAME, though only comprise 14% of the country (19). Black men spend a greater proportion of their original sentence in prison than other ethnicities (20). The disproportionality is particularly troubling for youth offenders, with rates rising from 25% of youth prisoners in 2006 to 41% in 2016 (21). Regarding religion, Muslims account for 4.2% of the population but 13.4% of the prison population (22).

Figure 4.1 from the Ministry of Justice and the Office for National Statistics highlights the breakdown in each criminal justice setting in relation to males and ethnicity (23).

Research indicates that the prevalence of mental disorders amongst individuals in the criminal justice system is higher than those in the general population (24, 25). For example, 23% of men in prison have suffered from anxiety or depression (1). This is particularly pertinent given recent reports that indicate the criminal justice system provides inadequate support for those with mental health issues (26). Research conducted by Tyler et al. found that women in prison were more likely than men to have been diagnosed with a personality disorder, anxiety disorder or mood disorder (14). Though, men were more likely to have been diagnosed with post-traumatic stress disorder, a psychiatric disorder, and autism spectrum conditions. People with learning disabilities, autism and attention-deficit/hyperactivity disorder are overrepresented in the criminal justice system (27, 28). Additionally, the Prison Reform Trust (1) conclude that '20–30% of all offenders have learning disabilities of difficulties that interfere with their ability to cope with the criminal justice system'.

There are five purposes of sentencing as contained in section 142 of the Criminal Justice Act 2003 (29) which the judicial system have to consider. These are:

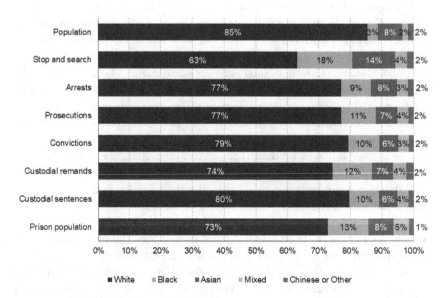

FIGURE 4.1 Ethnicity in the criminal justice system

- Punishment of offenders
- Reduction of crime (including its reduction by deterrence)
- Reform and rehabilitation of offenders
- Protection of the public
- Making of reparations by offenders to persons affected by their offences

This therefore means when considering reform and rehabilitation, offenders working on their alcohol use whilst in prison is important to help achieve this aim.

Men in prison

The USA has the highest prisoner rate in the world with around 639 prisoners per 100,000 of the national population (30). The USA also has the largest number of prisoners at around 2.12 million incarcerated in 2020 (30). African Americans make up the largest share of prisoners in US prisons. In 2018, there were almost 409,600 black, non-Hispanic prisoners compared to 394,800 white, non-Hispanic prisoners (30). Drug-related offenses are the most common cause of imprisonment followed by felonies such as murder and robbery (30).

Since about the year 2000, the world prison population total has grown by 24%, which is slightly less than the estimated increase in the world's general population over the same period (28%) (31). There is considerable variation between and within continents (31). However, prison population rates vary considerably between different regions of the world, and between different parts of the same continent (31). It has been reported that there are more than 2 million prisoners in the United States of America, 1.69 million in China (plus unknown numbers in pre-trial detention and other forms of detention), 811,000 in Brazil, 478,000 in India, 471,000 in the Russian Federation, 309,000 in Thailand, 291,000 in Turkey, 266,000 in Indonesia, 220,000 in Mexico, 189,000 in Iran and 165,000 in the Philippines (31).

There are 117 prisons in the UK that hold male prisoners, 104 run by the government and 13 ran by different private companies such as G4S or Serco. These prisons are categorised A-D unlike female prisons which are either open or closed. Category A prisons hold the most severe sentences, whilst category D are open settings. In addition, remand prisons hold those males who are waiting adjudication. In England and Wales, His Majesty's Prison and Probation Service and the Ministry of Justice are responsible for the publicly run prisons.

Male prisons are often the most overcrowded establishments (32). In addition to this, they are also often the oldest estates built in the Victorian era, making them least fit for purpose. More recent criminologists have considered the growing trend of exploring how designing prisons more effectively in a way to achieve reform and rehabilitation (32). Jewkes argues that such reform can have a profound physiological and psychological impact on those who work and live within prison establishments (33).

Following the abolishment of death penalty in 1965, imprisonment is the most serious punishment that can be imposed by a court in the UK (32). Although custodial sentences in prison are only used in approximately 7% of all criminal offences, it is important to reiterate that approximately 83,000 people are deprived of their liberty as a result of imprisonment (34).

In 2021, there were 74,981 men in prison in the UK, making up 95% of the entire prison population (34). The latest statistics reveal that there are approximately 80,000 men and 3,000 women in prison in England and Wales, suggesting a rise to 96% (3).

Men in prison face similar issues to women in that the prevalence of self-harm, suicide rates and assaults are rising (35). With 537 self-harm incidents per 1,000 male prisoners in the UK, there is a need to intervene with some of the issues males in prison face. In 2021, 98% of deaths in custody were of men, with an increase in death by suicide from the previous year (36). Findings from the Office for National Statistics (37) indicate that the male prisoners were 3.7 times more likely than men in the general population to die by suicide.

The rates of assault in male prison estates in the UK in the last quarter was 5,012, an increase of 14% (35). In addition to this, the rate of serious assaults is higher among the male prison population, with 11% of assaults being categorised as serious (compared to 6% in the female estate) (35).

Greham Skyes first discussed what is known as the pains of imprisonment. Sykes argued that such psychological pains are just as barbaric as the old-fashioned methods of punishment inflicted upon the body (38). The pains of imprisonment in his view were loss of liberty, loss of goods and services, loss of heterosexual relationships, and issues with autonomy and security (38). Sykes furthermore stated that: 'Such attacks... are less easily seen than a sadistic beating, a pair of shackles on the floor, or the caged man on a treadmill, but the destruction of the psyche is no less fearful than bodily affliction' (38). The fact that the male establishments are more overcrowded (32), only emphasises these pains.

All of these inequalities and pains of imprisonment make it difficult to work on risky drinking because alcohol is bought and sold legally but is none the less a drug with toxic effects and carries dangers associated with intoxication, as well as dependence (39). However, when considered alongside recidivism rates and prevalence of alcohol use disorders, it is nonetheless important.

The National Institute for Health and Care Research (NIHR) Public Health Research funded two-arm parallel group individually randomised prison pilot study of a male remand alcohol intervention for self-efficacy enhancement study (APPRAISE) (40) is a study that aimed to provide evidence for a future multi centre randomised controlled trial. The NIHR-funded APPRAISE study was developed after previous early feasibility and acceptability was explored in the Medical Research Council Public Health Intervention Development (MRC-PHIND) funded study PRISM-A (40, 41).

Men in prison and alcohol brief interventions

As mentioned, it has been shown that intervening to reduce alcohol use is cost-effective, generating both long- and short-term savings. Public Health England

(PHE) estimates, every £1 invested in effective alcohol treatment brings a social return of £5 (42). It has also been suggested that providing effective treatment is likely to significantly reduce the costs relating to alcohol as well as increase individual social welfare (43). However, as has been demonstrated, alcohol brief interventions within a prison setting is a relatively newly explored phenomenon. The few studies exploring this believe the environment could capitalise on the 'teachable moment' considered to be conducive to behaviour change, wherein those incarcerated can be encouraged to consider their alcohol use in context to their offending behaviour and the consequence of finding themselves in prison (44).

Experimental criminology research

Both authors of this chapter were involved in the aforementioned APPRAISE and PRISM-A studies (40, 41), as well as Dr Fergusons PhD work (45) that explored alcohol brief interventions with women in an open prison setting, building upon the two previous studies in the male estate. All studies aligned to the MRC framework (46). The relevant ethical approvals from University and HMPPS were obtained for all studies.

These research studies aimed to take a public health intervention into the criminal justice system, to assess the feasibility and acceptability of an alcohol brief intervention. Public health in recent years has aligned with social sciences and both now share similar aims (47). The ethos of public health has always been to do good, be useful and be civically constructive (48). Complex interventions are widely used in healthcare, public health and in areas of social policy (49). In healthcare, for example, an intervention can be used to address a purely health issue such as the issue of diabetes (50). Social policy interventions will consider issues such as school food policy (51). Whereas the more social determinants of health are addressed in public health interventions, with interventions tackling issues such as education, housing or crime (50). Within the criminal justice system, and prison specifically, complex interventions are a relatively new phenomenon.

PRISM-A was a mixed methods study that developed and refined a self-efficacy enhancing alcohol intervention within a prison setting (41). The study involved the views of the men within two prisons, as well as relevant staff and stakeholders. Men in the study were screened for potential alcohol use disorders using the ten-question Alcohol Use Disorders Test (AUDIT). A high prevalence was established (82% scored more than 8 on the AUDIT) highlighting what the evidence already shows about the prevalence of risky drinking amongst men in the criminal justice system. The study also provided evidence that it was possible to access, recruit consent and identify those individuals across the two prisons who were risky drinkers. It also established the willingness of staff to help with the access and recruitment of male remand prisoners. Twenty-four men were interviewed using semi-structured interviews and there was a strong consensus that they would be willing in a hypothetical situation to be followed up at 6 and 12 months as part of a research study. It is these findings alongside the dearth of evidence that lead to the APPRAISE study.

The APPRAISE study focused solely on those men on remand and used the intervention developed in PRISM-A. The research showed that addressing alcohol harm in prisons with those on remand can capitalise on the 'teachable moment' as the opportunity allows the men to address their alcohol use, whilst other inequalities are minimised (40). Men who enter the prisons on remand may suddenly find themselves with access to healthcare that they otherwise would or do not access.

The APPRAISE study successfully recruited 132 male remand prisoners into the study. The aim was 180, however the COVID-19 pandemic started during the trial. The aim was to recruit the men, and if possible, to recruit them, then deliver the alcohol brief intervention to those in the intervention arm (in this instance 53 out of 68 interventions were delivered in prison) and then follow up all 132 men at 12 months post intervention. Follow up with this population is extremely difficult and coupled with the COVID-19 pandemic, only 18 men were followed up. One of the learning outcomes from this study was that we need to further identify the best way to locate men once released from prison, in order to measure the effect of the intervention on the drinking levels of the men.

Chapter summary

This chapter has explored the prevalence of alcohol use disorders in relation to men in the criminal justice system. Males involved in the criminal justice system face inequalities in society and these have been highlighted within this chapter. A breakdown of the demographics of those men involved with the criminal justice system at various points has also been discussed. To highlight the specific issues faced when considering men in prison, the chapter has drawn upon recent relevant research that the authors took part in (40, 41). This aforementioned research explored alcohol use disorders with male remand prisoners. It is believed capitalising on the 'teachable moment' of finding oneself in prison can help with behaviour change. More research is needed in a COVID-19 free world.

References

1. Prison Reform Trust. Bromley briefings prison fact file, autumn 2014 ; 2014. Available from: https://prisonreformtrust.org.uk/publication/factfile-december-2010/
2. Department for Education. Outcomes for looked after children as of March 2011. London; 2011. www.gov.uk/government/statistics/outcomes-for-children-in-need-including-children-looked-after-by-local-authorities-in-england-2020-to-2021
3. Ministry of Justice. Prison population figures: 2022. Available from: www.gov.uk/government/publications/prison-population-figures-2022.2022
4. BMJ. BMJ best practice: Alcohol use disorder; 2018. Available from: https://bestpractice.bmj.com/topics/en-gb/198

5. Drummond C, Oyefeso, N, Phillips, T, Cheeta, S, Deluca, P, Winfield, H, Jenner, JH, Cobain, K, Galea, S, Saunders, V, Perryman, K, Fuller, T, Pappalardo, D, Baker, O, Christopolous, A, Alcohol needs assessment research project (ANARP): the 2004 national alcohol needs assessment for England. London: Department of Health, 2005.

6. Anderson P, Møller L, Galea G, WHO Regional Office for Europe. Alcohol in the European Union. Consumption, harm and policy approaches. Copenhagen: WHO Regional Office for Europe; 2012. p. 70.

7. Anderson P, Møller L, Galea G. Alcohol in the European Union Consumption, harm and policy approaches. Copenhagen, Denmark: WHO Regional Office for Europe; 2012.

8. Perkins HW. Surveying the damage: a review of research on consequences of alcohol misuse in college populations. Journal of Studies on Alcohol Supplement. 2002;14:91–100.

9. Rehm J, Gmel G. Patterns of alcohol consumption and social consequences. Results from an 8-year follow-up study in Switzerland. Addiction. 1999;94(6):899–912.

10. Office National Statistics. Crime survey for England and Wales, violent crime and sexual offences – Alcohol – Related violence. London: ONS; 2013/14.

11. Newbury-Birch D, McGovern R, Birch J, O'Neill G, Kaner H, Sondhi A, et al. A rapid systematic review of what we know about alcohol use disorders and brief interventions in the criminal justice system. International Journal of Prisoner Health. 2016;12(1):57–70.

12. Fazel S, Baines P, Doll H. Substance abuse and dependence in prisoners: A systematic review. Addiction. 2006;101(2):181–91.

13. Parkes T, MacAskill S, Brooks O, Jepson R, Ahterton I, Doi L, et al. Prison health needs assessment for alcohol problems. Edinburgh: NHS Health Scotland; 2011.

14. Tyler N, Miles L, Karadag B, Rogers G. An updated picture of the mental health needs of male and female prisoners in the UK: Prevalence, comorbidity, and gender differences. Social Psychiatry and Psychiatric Epidemiology. 2019;(54):1143–52.

15. Dignan J, Cavadino M. Penal policy in comparative perspective. Criminal Justice Matters. 2007;70(1):15–6.

16. Home Office. Police powers and procedures: Stop and search and arrests, England and Wales, year ending 31 March 2022 ; 2022. Available from: www.gov.uk/gov ernment/statistics/police-powers-and-procedures-stop-and-search-and-arrests-england-and-wales-year-ending-31-march-2022/police-powers-and-procedures-stop-and-search-and-arrests-england-and-wales-year-ending-31-march-2022

17. Ministry of Justice. Probation data; 2022. Available from: https://data.justice.gov. uk/probation

18. Lammy Review. Lammy review: An independent review into the treatment of, and outcomes for, black, Asian, and minority ethnic individuals in the criminal justice system; 2017. Available from: https://assets.publishing.service.gov.uk/government/ uploads/system/uploads/attachment_data/file/643001/lammy-review-final-rep ort.pdf

19. Ministry of Justice. NOMS annual offender equalities report: 2015 to 2016; 2016. Available from: www.gov.uk/government/statistics/noms-annual-offender-equalit ies-report-2015-to-2016

20. Ministry of Justice. Proven reoffending statistics: October to December 2018; 2020. Available from: www.gov.uk/government/statistics/proven-reoffending-statistics-october-to-december-2018

21. Ministry of Justice. Youth Justice Board, youth custody data, table 2.6; 2017. Available from: www.gov.uk/government/publications/youth-custody-data

22. Mullen J. Improving outcomes for young black and/or Muslim men in the Criminal Justice System. 2014. Available from: www.prisonpolicy.org/scans/young_review/improving_outcomes.pdf.2014

23. Ministry of Justice, Office of National Statistics. Ethnicity proportions for adults through the criminal justice system; 2020. Available from www.gov.uk/governm ent/statistics/ethnicity-and-the-criminal-justice-system-statistics-2020/ethnicity-and-the-criminal-justice-system-2020

24. Rebbapragada N, Furtado V, Hawker-Bond GW. Prevalence of mental disorders in prisons in the UK: A systematic review and meta-analysis. BJPsych Open. 2021;7(S1):S283–S284. doi:10.1192/bjo.2021.755

25. Brown P, Bakolis I, Appiah-Kusi E, Hallett N, Hotopf M, Blackwood N. Prevalence of mental disorders in defendants at criminal court. BJPsych Open. 2022;8(3):1–8.

26. Criminal Justice Joint Inspection. Criminal justice system failing people with mental health issues – with not enough progress over the past 12 years; 2021. Available from: www.justiceinspectorates.gov.uk/cjji/media/press-releases/2021/11/mental health2021/

27. ARC England. People with learning disabilities in the criminal justice system: A guide for carers and learning disability services; 2016. Available from: https://arcuk. org.uk/wp-content/uploads/2016/04/PWLD-in-the-CJS-Guide.pdf

28. Young J, Adamou M, Bolea B, Gudjonsson G, Muller U, Pitts M, et al. The identification and management of ADHD offenders within the criminal justice system: A consensus statement from the UK Adult ADHD Network and criminal justice agencies. BMC Psychiatry. 2011;11:32. https://doi.org/10.1186/1471-244X-11-32

29. Criminal Justice Act, (2003).

30. Statista. Crime worldwide – Statistics & facts 2022; 2022. Available from: www.stati sta.com/topics/780/crime/#dossierContents__outerWrapper

31. Fair H, Walmsley R. World prison population list thirteenth edition. USA: Institute for Crime and Justice Policy Research; 2021.

32. Harrison K. Penology: Theory, policy and practice. London: Red Globe Press; 2020.

33. Jewkes Y. Just design: Healthy prisons and the architecture of hope. Australian & New Zealand Journal of Criminology. 2018;51(3):319–38.

34. Ministry of Justice. Her Majesty's Prison and Probation Service. Prison population figures: 2021; 2021 . Available from: www.gov.uk/government/statistics/prison-population-figures-2021

35. Ministry of Justice, Office for National Statistics. Safety in custody statistics, England and Wales: Deaths in prison custody to September 2022 assaults and self-harm to June 2022. Gov.UK; 2022. Available from: www.gov.uk/government/statistics/safety-in-custody-quarterly-update-to-june-2022/safety-in-custody-statistics-england-and-wales-deaths-in-prison-custody-to-september-2022-assaults-and-self-harm-to-june-2022

36. Ministry of Justice. Safety in custody statistics, England and Wales: Deaths in prison custody to December 2021, assaults, and self-harm to September 2021. Gov.UK; 2022. Available from: www.gov.uk/government/statistics/safety-in-custody-quarte rly-update-to-september-2021/safety-in-custody-statistics-england-and-wales-deaths-in-prison-custody-to-december-2021-assaults-and-self-harm-to-septem ber-2021

37. Office for National Statistics. Male prisoners are 3.7 times more likely to die from suicide than the public; 2019. Available from: www.ons.gov.uk/news/news/malepr isonersare37timesmorelikelytodiefromsuicidethanthepublic

38. Sykes G. The society of captives: A study of a maximum-security prison. New Jersey: Princeton University Press; 1958.
39. Babor T, Caetano R, Casswell S, Edwards G, Giesbrecht N, Graham K, et al. Alcohol: No ordinary commodity: Research and public policy. Revista Brasileira de Psiquiatria. 2010;26(4):280–3.
40. Holloway A, Guthrie V, Waller G, Smith J, Boyd J, Mercado S, et al. A two-arm parallel-group individually randomised prison pilot study of a male remand alcohol intervention for self-efficacy enhancement: The APPRAISE study protocol. BMJ Open. 2021;11:e040636. doi: 10.1136/bmjopen-2020-040636
41. Holloway A, Landale S, Ferguson J, Newbury-Birch D, Parker R, Smith P, et al. Alcohol Brief Interventions (ABIs) for male remand prisoners: Protocol for development of a complex intervention and feasibility study (PRISM-A). BMJ Open. 2017;7(4):e014561.
42. Public Health England. Alcohol and drugs prevention, treatment and recovery: Why invest? 2015. Available from: www.gov.uk/government/publications/alcohol-and-drug-prevention-treatment-and-recovery-why-invest/alcohol-and-drug-prevention-treatment-and-recovery-why-invest
43. Raistrick D, Heather N, Godfrey C. Review of the effectiveness of treatment for alcohol problems. London: National Treatment Agency for Substance Misuse, UK; 2006.
44. Babor T, De La Fuente J, Saunders J, Grant M. AUDIT, the Alcohol Use Disorders Identification Test, guidelines for use in primary health care. Geneva: World Health Organization; 1989.
45. Ferguson J, Leese M. Women, the pains of imprisonment and public health interventions. In: Masson I, Booth N (eds.) The Routledge handbook of women's experiences of criminal justice. London: Routledge; 2022. pp. 452–63.
46. Medical Research Council. A framework for development and evaluation of RCT's for complex interventions to improve health. London: MRC; 2000.
47. Petticrew M, Whitehead M, Macintyre SJ, Graham H, Egan M. Evidence for public health policy on inequalities: 1: The reality according to policymakers. Journal of Epidemiology and Community Health. 2004;58(10):811–6.
48. Viseltear AJ. The ethos of public health. Journal of Public Health Policy. 1990;11(2):146–50.
49. Petticrew M. When are complex interventions 'complex'? When are simple interventions 'simple'? European Journal of Public Health. 2011;21(4):397–8.
50. Lysdahl KB, Hofmann B. Complex health care interventions: Characteristics relevant for ethical analysis in health technology assessment. GMS Health Technology Assessment. 2016;12. doi: 10.3205/hta000124. PMID: 27066147; PMCID: PMC4811193.
51. Moore GF, Evans RE, Hawkins J, Littlecott H, Melendez-Torres GJ, Bonell C, et al. From complex social interventions to interventions in complex social systems: Future directions and unresolved questions for intervention development and evaluation. Evaluation. 2018;25(1):23–45.

5

RISKY DRINKING AMONGST WOMEN IN THE CRIMINAL JUSTICE SYSTEM

Introduction: why a gendered approach?

There are currently 3,641 women in prison in the UK compared to 80,000 men (4.6%). This is across only 12 prisons in the UK, with only one in Scotland and none in Wales (1). Significantly more females are found to be risky drinkers when they arrive in prison (24%) compared to their male counterparts (18%) (2). Moreover, individuals in the criminal justice system, particularly women, are much more likely to suffer from inequalities in society. For women this leads to gendered pains of imprisonment (loss of contact with family; power, autonomy and control; psychological well-being and mental health; matters of trust, privacy and intimacy) (3).

To date, there is a dearth of evidence in relation to delivering alcohol screening and brief interventions in the criminal justice system, specifically to women. This chapter will explore the feasibility and acceptability of alcohol screening and brief intervention for females in prison in great detail and discuss recent research by the author that added to the evidence base by making recommendations for a future pilot study of alcohol screening and brief intervention with women in prison. The research aforementioned suggests that delivering a public health intervention and underpinning the research with criminological theory (pains of imprisonment) could help women capitalise on the 'teachable moment' necessary to induce behaviour change. To date, there is no research in the prison setting that tailors *any* intervention for women based on both public health (behaviour change) and criminological theory (pains of imprisonment).

This chapter will discuss the prevalence of risky drinking amongst women in the criminal justice system. The contextual background of women in prison will set the scene for why separating the issue of male and female drinking in the criminal justice system is necessary. To do so, statistics will be included, and

DOI: 10.4324/9781003169802-5

the gendered pains of imprisonment will be discussed in this chapter to give context as to why looking at risky drinking in women is difficult but necessary to manage. Throughout this chapter, an exploration of why a more holistic approach is necessary when working with women in prison will be explored.

Women and alcohol

Prevalence

As discussed in previous chapters, the prevalence of alcohol use disorders within the criminal justice system is noticeably higher than that of the general population (4). A review of such prevalence found that up to 63% of women in the UK criminal justice system scored positive for an alcohol use disorder (4). When looking specifically at prison, the prevalence of those scoring positive for an alcohol use disorder is between 51 and 63% (4). This compares to 24% of the general population in the UK (5, 6).

Risky drinking and women

A more obvious factor for a gendered approach is the biological differences between men and women (7). Prisons only hold two types of estate, male and female, and this is determined by biological sex. Biological differences between male and female anatomy mean that women process alcohol differently to men due to differences in body water mass, as well as differing metabolism (7). The hormonal differences in women's bodies can also cause women to become intoxicated at a quicker speed, especially prior to menstruation (8). Because alcohol screening and brief intervention is based on patterns of drinking and associated risk (9), these biological factors become relevant when considering intervention.

In addition to patterns of risky drinking, when looking at a gendered approach, it is important to explore the reasons women are drinking. Within the criminal justice system, due to social inequalities, it may be that women are drinking to hide pain from things that have happened in their lives (3). The next section explores some of the issues that women face, that could contribute to risky drinking.

Women in prison

It is known that the prison system was designed by men, for men and is often inadequate to fulfil the needs of women (10). The Bromley Briefings Report (11) noted that women make up 15% of probation caseload and as mentioned, currently make up less than 5% of the entire prison population. With an average of 13,641 women being imprisoned each year in England and Wales (12), it is important to note that the average cost per prisoner in 2019 was £41,136, this includes closed, local and open prisons (13). This amount is rising each year, with a £3,593 increase per prisoner since the 2017/18 expenditures (13).

However, given the vulnerable nature of females who enter the criminal justice system, and prison specifically, when trying to induce behaviour change, it is imperative to consider these vulnerabilities. Exactly ten years apart, in 2007 and 2017 welcomed the published reports by Baroness Corston (14, 15). The Corston reports were published when Baroness Corston was horrified at the state of HMP Holloway Women's prison. Highlighted in the second report was that, according to the Crime Survey of England and Wales (16), women are more likely to be subject to abuse as children, particularly sexual assault. The report also states that women are more likely to self-harm in prison and self-harm more frequently than male prisoners. The prevalence of women in prison who have reported experiencing emotional, physical or sexual abuse as a child is frightenly high, 53% (compared to 27% men) (17). Women in prison take up 25% of all self-harm incidents, even though they only make up 5% of the overall prison population (17). In 2019, self-harm per individual was over twice as high for females compared to males (9.3 instances compared to 4.4) (18). Aside from past harm and current mental state, women are often the primary carers for dependent young children. Being separated from them when imprisoned makes the prison experience significantly different for women than men, this is then compounded because there are only a small number of women's prisons meaning that women tend to be located further away from their homes, making it difficult to maintain family ties, receive regular visits and be resettled back into the community.

The Prison Reform Trust reported that family contact is crucial to rehabilitating female prisoners, however, the average distance for women is about 64 miles (and often actually more) (11) due to the small number of women's prisons. This distance inevitably affects the number of visits women will receive from family and can impact on their opportunities to go home on release on temporary licence if they are in an open prison. This can contribute to women experiencing what Aiello and McQueeney (2016: 54) (19) described as, 'an invisible form of gendered punishment'. Women in prison can face a multiplicity of factors that impact on their journey through the prison system, but it is important to remember that they are not passive victims, they remain as active agents, with the capacity to shape their present and future with the appropriate support (3). In England and Wales, it is estimated that 17,240 children a year are separated from their mothers due to the mothers being imprisoned, however, the actual number is not known as this information is not systematically recorded (20); this undoubtedly will have an effect on such rehabilitation and any work the women take part in whilst imprisoned.

From the literature, it is clear that treating women and men equally does not merely mean giving both men and women the same treatment:

> Equal treatment for men and women is a matter of approach not outcome. The underlying assumption is that fairness consists of people in similar circumstances being treated in similar ways, but it must be recognised that men and women do not necessarily appear in similar circumstances
>
> (21)

The Equality Act (2007) was brought into legislation highlighting this issue and gave precedent for a new gender duty that means that women and men should be treated with equivalent respect, according to need. This results in different services and policies being required for men and women to embrace fairness, but also inclusivity. Whilst the focus is usually on the fact that women are not treated equally given all of their aforementioned differences, it is important but not the only point to consider. It is still important to note that women are victimised and this is often focused upon in detail in research (18, 22). However, 'Women as victims' tends to overshadow the fact that women are also offenders and more often than not, they can be both a victim and an offender (18, 23).

Pains of imprisonment

In addition to the vulnerabilities discussed, scholars have identified a number of pains of imprisonment that can be experienced by both male and female prisoners. These pains were first described by Sykes in 1958 who stated that although society had moved on from an environment in which physical pain and torture were being used as punishment, the psychological pain of imprisonment was just as damaging to an individual (24). More recently, Crewe et al. described what has become known as gendered pains of imprisonment (3). These are losing contact, power, autonomy and control, mental health and physical well-being, trust, privacy and intimacy (3); again highlighting the vulnerable nature of women in prison and the need to consider this when tailoring interventions. This also highlights how the nature of women's imprisonment, for example, being held at considerable distance from loved ones, can exacerbate the pains of imprisonment.

Recent work by author (JF)

With the increased interest in experimental criminology, interventions have more recently been introduced in various trials and pilot studies, and mostly in the USA (25). The work recently carried out by the author (JF) as part of a PhD study explored qualitatively how feasible and acceptable it is to women in prison and relevant staff and stakeholders, to deliver such an intervention for alcohol within an open prison. This work considered all of the points noted thus far within this chapter, and the work was designed with public health (behaviour change) theory and criminological theory (pains of imprisonment).

The qualitative part of the study took place in a women's open prison in the Northeast of England with residents of the prison, staff and stakeholders. All participants were given a copy of the AUDIT screening tool and an infographic of the intervention itself. The experiences of the female residents indicated that the concept of the 'journey' into and out of prison is an important consideration when assessing the feasibility and acceptability of an alcohol screening and brief intervention with this population of women. Close analysis of the transcripts led to the identification of five main themes, the first four being an exploration of the women's journey which gave context to the more pragmatic elements of the proposed delivery itself, and the fifth being the pragmatic points that helped develop a future study. The contextual themes are discussed below in turn.

A woman's journey into prison – 'I really wasn't bothered about coming to prison, at the time it was like a relief' (015)

Participants reflected upon the chaotic lifestyles of the women prior to entering the prison, talking about past trauma, alcohol and drug abuse, and poor family relationships. The interviews showed a need to explore these points and understand their lives on the outside in order to deliver the intervention in a way that will have an impact despite of this, as the likelihood is, the women will return to this way of life upon release. The impact of trauma was prominent, and many women discussed their traumatic childhoods and in some cases traumatic adulthoods as victims of abuse. For some prison was almost a positive shift in their lives, and others went further to suggest that their traumatic relationships had in fact contributed to them being sent to prison.

Given the difficult and chaotic life that was normal for some of the participants prior to prison, it is important to consider what this means in relation to the feasibility and acceptability of the alcohol screening and brief intervention. Understanding the pain and suffering that some of the women have experienced prior to entering prison is particularly important when considering this type of alcohol screening and brief intervention. If, as some of the participants suggested, that prison offers some women a period of respite, then it would suggest that this would be a good time for the intervention. Staff confirmed the fragility of the women when they enter prison, and they highlighted that (in their opinion) mental health was an issue for 80–90% of the residents in their care. When exploring suitable interventions, it is essential to remember the women's vulnerability and the fact that they are likely to go back to what can be a difficult and chaotic life. When considering this context, it is likely that support on release should be built into any intervention.

The impact of their drinking varied but one woman stated that if she had not ended up in prison, she would have killed herself drinking because all she did was drink and she prioritised this over eating. This is another example of understanding the context of the women's life prior to, during and on release from the prison. The participants suggested that drinking alcohol was a 'normal' part of their lives at that point but for some their views changed during this journey through prison. As well as the amount of alcohol drank, women talked about the implications of this drinking. One of the participants suggested that alcohol was responsible for most women being in prison. She went on to suggest that they ended up in custody because they were either in a rut, 'drunk and stupid', or stealing to fund an addiction.

> its why I ended up in jail. If I hadn't of gone out, I wouldn't have been in jail (018)

However, whilst it was acknowledged by some women that they were in prison for drinking alcohol at risky levels, it was evident in their interviews that the reason they drank alcohol in this risky way was often due to something that had happened to them, or some sort of abuse or trauma. It was interesting that they did not always make this link themselves, and as mentioned above, many women simply viewed alcohol as the reason for their prison sentence, and not this trauma. These reasons ranged from abuse to losing custody of their children, and during the interviews some women were visibly upset when talking about these issues.

> ...and I lost custody of me kids, and then I just had, a drink, you know, because it made me feel better.... And then as time went on, I was drinking like, soon as I got up in the morning (019)

Staff described two separate groups of women within the estate: those where you can clearly see a link between their drinking and offending, for example, a woman who is consistently very intoxicated and one day stabs her partner; and second, a woman like 'me and you' who does not necessarily drink within the recommended daily guidelines but their use is unlikely to affect their release on temporary licence because the temptation does not pose any more of a risk than it would without having the intervention in place. This raises an interesting point given the intended audience of alcohol screening and brief interventions because the target audience would be the second type of woman the staff member describes. Screening every woman therefore would fill this gap in the current regime and help provide a service to women in the prison who potentially do not even know they need it.

The journey through prison as a woman – 'Still now, still now I could go back to a closed prison and I'd probably find it easier' (005)

Participants reflected upon their time in the closed prison and discussed the differences in the open estate. Most importantly, this gave context to why an intervention may be delivered better at a certain time throughout the woman's journey. The residents and staff also reflected upon any services women engage with in relation to their alcohol use whilst they are in prison.

To progress to an open prison estate can take many years and those serving long sentences often strive to reach this point in order gain more freedom. Despite the fact that this transition is long sought after, and anticipated as a positive move, the women in this study noted how this change brought with it some unforeseen challenges. The women talked about how much being in the open estate meant to them once they had settled, but they noted that it was extremely difficult for them when they first arrived. This was apparent in the interviews with both staff and residents. These reasons ranged from concern about who to trust, to feeling that they were overwhelmed by the amount of information they were given on arrival. The women also identified that although the move was positive, there were still things that they found difficult. One of the most talked about difficulties with this transition to open prison was the bureaucracy of the transition itself. Women talked about endless induction activities and having to go back to sharing a room because most of them had been living in single cells when in closed conditions, meaning a loss in privacy.

> you get dragged everywhere in that first week, you just get dragged to all these different inductions, and all these different (015)

If women feel overwhelmed with information upon arrival, it suggests that this is not the best time to introduce alcohol screening and brief interventions and waiting a period of time is key to acceptability of them. The change to the open prison for many resulted in them feeling that instead of taking an important step forward, they feel like they have actually regressed.

> ...and then I come here and took a complete step back (015)

It is therefore important to consider the emotional state of the women when they reach the open estate. If the women have more immediate needs upon arrival to the prison, the intervention would not be considered as a priority to them, and without them wanting to make a change, the intervention would have little effect (26). One woman highlighted the difficulty of the transition by explaining that although there are more freedoms awarded in the open estate, it actually made it more difficult to adjust.

It is well evidenced that women in prison can experience issues with trust (3) but it is interesting to note that previous research has often been centred around the trust the women have in others, rather than on the trust placed upon them (3, 27–29). One woman highlighted how she felt on arrival:

> [It was] 'overwhelming [about] how unsecure it is here' (001)

This is particularly significant with the type of intervention because part of the acceptability and feasibility is important to identify who is in the most acceptable role to deliver the brief advice. The consensus in this study was that it should be the personal officer who is a prison officer who each prisoner has assigned to them who delivers the alcohol screening and brief intervention. This was one of the most surprising findings because it was very different to the findings in previous work in the male estate (30).

These findings suggest that due to the time it takes to adjust to the new freedoms offered as part of transitioning into the open estate, coupled with the shift in trust and the adjustments necessary there, waiting a period of time before offering an intervention is necessary. It also appears that because of this new trust and change in relationships between prison officers and residents, utilising this relationship in order to deliver the intervention would be a cost-effective way to deliver brief alcohol interventions within this setting. The findings suggest that the women start to shift their mentality towards thinking about the outside when they reach the open estate, suggesting an opportunistic time to be approached with the short intervention.

Influences on a woman in prisons decision-making – 'And he's like 'mum, I've gotta say, you are a better version of yourself'.... So even they see all that' (016)

To further explore the acceptability of the intervention, and the fact that the intervention is underpinned by behaviour change and the women reaching a 'teachable moment' (31), it became apparent that what is important is what influences the women in prison to make certain decisions regarding behaviour. This meant understanding what is important to a woman in prison and what does she consider when making a decision. Two main factors emerged within this are the element of family influences and staff rapport.

When carrying out the AUDIT (31) with the women, the question that caused the strongest reaction with women was question 10, '*has a relative or friend or doctor or another health worker been concerned about your drinking or suggested you cut down?*' As expected, the main influence on a woman's decision-making when she reaches this point in her journey is any children she has. Interestingly, the data suggests that this is the case irrespective of whether the children are young or older, and in some cases the women may also have grandchildren to consider.

> so that does make you feel a bit guilty and then, the affect. I mean, even though my children are grown up, they're still my children (011)

The women talked openly about changing their drinking whilst in prison because they could see the effect it had on their children; something they could not see before their journey into prison. This reinforces the timing of the intervention being well suited in order to achieve the most out of the behaviour change element of the intervention (32). This concern for their children appeared to be reciprocated when women spoke of family members praising them for the positive changes they have made on their journey, this sparked a clear surge of confidence when the women opened up about it.

Staff discussed the importance of family to the women, highlighting the openness of the women in sharing their pain around missing their children and loved ones and some staff discussed how focusing on the fact that they miss them means they have something to strive to get out for.

> I think it's nice when they get out cos they go back to that, that somebody's still thinking about them (S001)

These are all important points to consider when tailoring such an intervention, particularly with using the full ten-question AUDIT (31) tool and considering it as an important component of the intervention and not simply a tool to assess prevalence. By asking them all ten questions, specifically question 10, it could be enough to inspire women, highlighting why it is important to make a change not only for themselves but for their relationships with loved ones.

One of the most positive elements of carrying out the interviews was the surprising responses about staff rapport from both the perspective of the residents in the prison and the staff. Residents openly spoke about how they would choose uniformed staff (prison staff such as prison officers) to disclose personal information, but this was in turn mirrored by the responses of prison staff, followed by shock when they learned the residents had said the same. This surprising finding is important to consider when deciding who should deliver the intervention. Previous work with men in prison has found that this feeling is not shared (33) and therefore it appears to be a gendered response.

As previously discussed, the women reflected very differently upon their time in the closed prison compared to their time in their current open conditions. This was strengthened further when they talked about the difference in their relationship with staff in the two estates. The women directly gave their feelings towards staff in the closed prison, with a resounding sense of mistrust and poor treatment. This was highlighted even more by the contrast in the rapport between residents and staff in the open prison.

> It's like they take a different tablet here (019)

> all of the staff are friendly and we talk to them about sensitive issues anyway...even uniformed (001)

Staff gave some context as to why the women have a better rapport in the open estate and this ranged from them being easier to approach, to the women being more confident. Women are carrying out activities themselves due to the freedoms granted and so they do not need to rely on staff in the same way as they do in closed, making room for a better relationship.

Staff were nevertheless cautious to admit there was a level playing field and that the relationship is still not one you may find in other settings. The women are there as a consequence of their behaviour and it is not as simple as other settings, nothing is truly confidential because it could pose a risk to the woman, other women or even staff or the community. There was as always reservations around timing and money, however, again, it appeared to be a barrier that could be overcome.

A woman's new journey when she leaves prison – "If I had been a drinker, the first thing I would have probably wanted....to ease me and calm me" (016)

Participants acknowledged the logistical difficulties women have when leaving prison. This theme explored how family relationships are affected upon leaving the prison system as well as the logistics involving issues such as housing. In-depth discussion was had around the woman's 'new journey', consisting of leaving the prison system and looking forward. Both residents and staff spoke profusely about identity transition through a resident's journey and what this means for the days ahead, as well as family relationships. Another element of discussion took place around the logistics of this new journey. Some women may have never been alone and therefore need to learn how to support themselves.

The women reaching the open estate and having no choice but to look forward appears to have allowed them to make those initial steps in repairing or rebuilding broken relationships on the outside. This is important to note as it can be drawn upon in the intervention and those relationships can form part of the intervention and change itself, again suggesting an ideal time for the intervention to take place. Alternatively, some women discussed leaving bad relationships since entering the prison system and explained feeling a sense of relief that they were leaving prison and not going back to those, suggesting that as well as rebuilding important relationships when being given the opportunity to reflect, they also use the opportunity to end relationships that are holding them back in some way.

> got rid of those demons (016)

Although it was discussed that women suffer greatly by leaving behind children and family when incarcerated, staff spoke of how this pain also encouraged those women throughout their journey. They suggested that having the family ties was positive when the women were leaving, as they have something to go back to, highlighting that these emotions faced by the women when they are in prison, are visible to staff.

> I think men are quite selfish prisoners whereas women come to prison and they're thinking about the men, their children you know who else they'll look after and when so and so depends on me, I'll look after, you know what I mean, they've got so many worries that I think it's nice when they get out cos they go back to that, that somebody's still thinking about them.
> *(S001)*

Staff being able to sense the women's emotions is beneficial when considering their rapport and the delivery of the intervention. To be able to discuss sensitive issues such as family during an intervention would have to be handled with care and the staff already having the knowledge of what the women are dealing with individually would be a facilitator in delivering the intervention and therefore more likely to induce change.

The main logistical issues residents discussed were related to alcohol, lack of available support from others and the location of where they are going out to. The women discussed alcohol openly and how often the anxiety of release on temporary licence can make someone want to drink alcohol, advancing the risk of drinking.

These are important findings to consider in relation to the intervention. This behaviour change element of this intervention relies on the women to make the change themselves and this data suggests that the women would need to rely on each other to support them through any change.

As well as the risk of easier access to alcohol, one of the main concerns the staff had was in relation to a lack of support for women once they leave the prison. These findings suggest that following women up as part of the intervention when they have left the prison would help them to know they are supported and bridge that gap a little in relation to alcohol.

> Yeah I think it's a good idea cos like you say it's about them knowing that you're still like supporting them even when they're out there... (S002)

All of the findings of this qualitative research led to the observation that women rarely leave the open prison as the same women who first entered the criminal justice system. This appears true of their alcohol use but also of their identities and highlighted in their new-found strength. Both women and staff talked about this shift in identity, and women commented on how their family had observed this too. It is interesting to note that the seriousness of their offending and their journey through prison is the cause for this positive shift in identity, the women themselves acknowledged this would not have occurred had they not been forced into looking at themselves.

Unexpectedly, this qualitative work found some women are grateful for their journey through the prison. The women did not say it was an easy journey, but one that meant they were grateful for the outcome.

So I've been grateful for the experience (O16)

The women were grateful for the experience because it had forced them to make a change. This change resulted in a shift in their identity. Resilience was at the heart of this identity shift and echoed in many of the women's comments. The women discussed being in prison making them a better people because they were put in a position where working on personal issues was not only a possibility but was encouraged. This is important in considering why this would be a good setting to deliver the alcohol brief intervention as it would fit in to this 'working on themselves'.

At the heart of this identity, transition and new-found resilience appeared to be trauma in the past. It is a safe prediction that many of the women would have ended up in worse situations if prison had not removed them from their previous lives. Women discussed their alcohol use, but also trauma in relation to past relationships. Women described a shift in their ways of thinking that was caused by finding them in prison. It is evident that prison became a teachable moment in their lives. The women downplayed the seriousness of the trouble in their pre-prison lives but talked about the situation with a sense of only being able to talk about it in such a way because they have come through 'the other side'.

Chapter summary

This chapter has explored the prevalence of risky drinking amongst women in the criminal justice system, with a more specific focus on women in prison. What has been demonstrated is that it is necessary to consider women separately to men, and tailoring interventions based upon the gendered pains of imprisonment is a manageable way to do so. By using a more holistic approach, interventions can be targeted and tailored in a way that will home in on what is considered a 'teachable moment'.

References

1. Gov.uk. Her Majesty's Prison Service, Prison finder; 2021. www.gov.uk/governm ent/collections/prisons-in-england-and-wales
2. Newbury-Birch D, Ferguson J, Landale S, Giles EL, McGeechan GJ, Gill C, et al. A systematic review of the efficacy of alcohol interventions for incarcerated people. Alcohol and Alcoholism. 2018;53(4):412–25.
3. Crewe B, Hulley S, Wright S. The gendered pains of life imprisonment. British Journal of Criminology. 2017;57(6):1359–78.
4. Newbury-Birch D, McGovern R, Birch J, O'Neill G, Kaner H, Sondhi A, et al. A rapid systematic review of what we know about alcohol use disorders and brief interventions in the criminal justice system. International Journal of Prisoner Health. 2016;12(1):57–70.
5. Fazel S, Baines P, Doll H. Substance abuse and dependence in prisoners: A systematic review. Addiction. 2006;101(2):181–91.
6. Parkes T, MacAskill S, Brooks O, Jepson R, Ahterton I, Doi L, et al. Prison health needs assessment for alcohol problems. Edinburgh: NHS Health Scotland; 2011.
7. Wilsnack R, Vogeltanz N, Wilsnack S, Harris R. Gender differences in alcohol consumption and adverse drinking consequences: Cross-cultural patterns. Addiction. 2000;95(2):251–65.
8. Center for Substance Abuse Treatment. SAMHSA/CSAT treatment improvement protocols. Substance abuse treatment: Addressing the specific needs of women. Rockville, MD: Substance Abuse and Mental Health Services Administration (US); 2009.
9. Babor TF, Higgins-Biddle JC, Saunders JB, Monteiro MG. The alcohol use disorders identification test: Guidelines for use in primary care. Geneva: World Health Organization; 2002.
10. Wyld C, Lomax P, Collinge T. Understanding women's pathways through the criminal justice system. Available from: www.thinknpc.org/resource-hub/understand ing-womens-pathways-through-the-criminal-justice-system/: NPC; 2018.
11. Prison Reform Trust. Bromley briefings prison factfile: Autumn 2017; 2016. Available from: www.prisonreformtrust.org.uk/Portals/0/Documents/Brom ley%20Briefings/old%20editions/Autumn%202017%20Factfile.pdf
12. Corke J. Women in prison, from a critical analysis of female imprisonment towards a female centred approach to penology. University of Hull, 2019. Available from: https://crimsoc.hull.ac.uk/2020/06/24/women-in-prison/
13. Ministry of Justice. Her Majesty's Prison and Probation Service. HMPPS annual Digest 2018/2019. Prison Performance. Ministry of Justice; 2019. Available from: https://assets.publishing.service.gov.uk/government/uploads/system/uplo ads/attachment_data/file/747823/annual-hmpps-digest-2017-18.pdf

14. Corston J. The Corston report. Home Office; 2007. Available from: https://web archive.nationalarchives.gov.uk/20130206102659;www.justice.gov.uk/publicati ons/docs/corston-report-march-2007.pdf

15. Corston J. The Corston report, 10 years on, how far have we come on the road to reform for women affected by the criminal justice system? London: Barrow Cadbury Trust; 2017.

16. Crime in England and Wales: year ending September 2017; 2017. Available from: www.ons.gov.uk/peoplepopulationandcommunity/crimeandjustice/bulletins/ crimeinenglandandwales/yearendingseptember2017

17. Ministry of Justice. Offender Management Statistics Bulletin, England and Wales. England and Wales: Ministry of Justice; 2015.

18. Ministry of Justice. Office for National Statistics. Statistics on Women and the Criminal Justice System 2019. Ministry of Justice and Office of National Statistics; 2020.https://assets.publishing.service.gov.uk/government/uploads:

19. Aiello B, McQueeney K. How can you live without your kids? Distancing from and embracing the stigma of 'incarcerated mother'. Journal of Prison Education and Reentry. 2016;3(1):32–49.

20. Wilks-Wiffen S. Voice of a child London. London: Howard League for Penal Reform; 2011.

21. Hedderman C, Gelsthorpe L. Understanding the sentencing of women. London: Home Office; 1997.

22. Reno J, Marcus D, Leary M, Samuels J. In: U.S. Department of Justice (ed.) Research on women and girls in the justice system. Washington DC: National Institute of Justice; 2000.

23. Barberet R. Women, crime and criminal justice. New York: Routledge; 2014.

24. Sykes G. The society of captives: A study of a maximum-security prison. New Jersey: Princeton University Press; 1958.

25. Welsh BC, Braga AA, Bruinsma GJ. Experimental criminology: Prospects for advancing science and public policy. Cambridge, UK: Cambridge University Press; 2013.

26. Prochaska JO, Di Clemente CC. Transtheoretical therapy: Toward a more integrative model of change. Psychotherapy. 1982;19(3):276–88.

27. Burkhart KW. Women in prison. Oxford, England: Doubleday; 1973. p. viii, 465–viii.

28. Severance TA. "You know who you can go to": Cooperation and exchange between incarcerated women. Prison Journal (Philadelphia, PA). 2005;85(3):343–67.

29. Greer K. Walking an emotional tightrope: Managing emotions in a women's prison. Symbolic Interaction. 2002;25(1):117–39.

30. Holloway A, Guthrie V, Waller G, Smith J, Boyd J, Mercado S, et al. A two-arm parallel-group individually randomised prison pilot study of a male remand alcohol intervention for self-efficacy enhancement: The APPRAISE study protocol. BMJ Open. 2021;11(4):e040636.

31. Babor T, De La Fuente J, Saunders J, Grant M. AUDIT, the Alcohol Use Disorders Identification Test, guidelines for use in primary health care. Geneva: World Health Organization; 1989.

32. Heather N, Hönekopp J. A revised edition of the Readiness to Change Questionnaire [Treatment Version]. Addiction Research & Theory. 2009;16(5):421–33.

33. Holloway A, Landale S, Ferguson J, Newbury-Birch D, Parker R, Smith P, et al. Alcohol Brief Interventions (ABIs) for male remand prisoners: Protocol for development of a complex intervention and feasibility study (PRISM-A). BMJ Open. 2017;7(4):e014561.

6

RISKY DRINKING AND BRIEF INTERVENTIONS FOR YOUNG PEOPLE IN THE CRIMINAL JUSTICE SYSTEM

Introduction

As shown in previous chapters, alcohol harm and the harms related to it are a significant issue across the world. However, it has been shown that there is a complex interplay between individual and contextual factors and risky drinking behaviours and alcohol-related crime (1).

Adolescence is a critical developmental stage where young people make behavioural and lifestyle choices that have the potential to impact on their health and well-being into adulthood. While risk-taking is important for healthy psychological development for many, inappropriate risk-taking is significantly associated with health and social harm during adolescence and these harms persist well into adulthood (2, 3). Young people are much more vulnerable than adults to the adverse effects of substance use due to a range of physical and psychological factors that often interact and the differential impact of substances on the developing brain (4–6). In addition to an increased risk of accidents and injury (7), substance use in young people is also associated with poor educational performance and exclusion from education. Over the academic year 2015–16, almost 10% of permanent school exclusions in state secondary schools were due to alcohol and substance use (8). In the longer term, substance use is also associated with increased prevalence of noncommunicable diseases, such as cancer, cardiovascular disease and gastrointestinal disorders (9, 10).

The number of young people who consume alcohol is declining, although those who do drink tend to drink more. In 2018, 54% of those aged 14 and 69% aged 15 consumed alcohol and 23% had consumed alcohol in the past week (11). The mean weekly alcohol consumption for males at aged 14 was 5 units and for those aged 15 it was 7 units, where 1 unit equals 10ml or 8g of pure ethanol. For females, this was 5.5 units and 5 units, respectively (11).

DOI: 10.4324/9781003169802-6

A recent study carried out in Accident Emergency Departments of England ascertained levels of risky drinking (3+ on the AUDIT-C tool) with young people aged 11–17 (12). Of the 3,327 surveyed 1,639 screened positive as a risky drinker (49%) (12). Of those randomised (*n* = 1,639), 8% had previous involvement with the police (12).

Giles et al. carried out a randomised controlled trial of alcohol screening and brief interventions with 14- to 15-year-olds in the high school setting (3). They used the Adolescent Single Alcohol Question (A-SAQ) which was shown to be a reliable single-screening question for drinking frequency in the Screening and Intervention Programme for Sensible Drinking (SIPS) research programme in adults (13–15). It is a modified version of the Single Alcohol Screening Question (M-SASQ) (16), which is adapted for adolescent alcohol consumption (17). They found that 24% of the young people scored positive as a risky drinker (3, 18).

While the relationship between criminal activity and alcohol use is complex (19, 20), there is clear evidence that the prevalence of substance use is far higher in the youth offending population than the general youth population (21). Data derived from the Youth Offending Team, ASSETPLUS in the UK, indicates that most young people in the criminal justice system use substances (76%) whilst 72% have a mental health need (22).

The Juvenile Cohort Study shows that 32% of young offenders score 2 or more on the ASSET tool for substance use, indicating substance use is at least in part a reason for them associating in criminal activity, and 12% score 3+ (23). While the relationship between substance use and criminal activity is complex, it is clearly a major issue in the youth offending population.

In the criminal justice system, substance use and offending are related in the context of other forms of disinhibitory behaviour, such as aggression and risk-taking (24, 25). Young people involved in the criminal justice system are a particularly vulnerable group, with a greater propensity to take risks that are likely to have long-term impact on their future health and well-being. This is because young offenders often lead chaotic lives and face complex problems, including substance use, unsuitable accommodation and emotional or mental health issues (26). Furthermore, literacy levels are very low within this population and the vast majority have in the past been excluded from school (27).

It has been shown that young people who offend experience a range of complex multiple risks and vulnerabilities including neglect and abuse (28, 29), substance use and related problems (30) and exclusion from school (31). Research has shown that young people who offend are more likely to experience a range of inequalities in later life, for example, worse physical health (30), early pregnancy (32) and higher rates of tobacco use and drug and alcohol dependence (31, 33, 34), economic hardship and reduced employment opportunities (35). There is widespread agreement that young people who offend are at increased risk of health and social problems, making them one of the most vulnerable populations (36). Epidemiological studies highlight the fact that, in common with other vulnerable groups of young people, such as the homeless and those in care, young offenders are a hard-to-reach group from a health needs perspective, only accessing physical and mental health services in times of crisis and accessing these services is often associated with involvement with other agencies (24, 34, 37, 38).

This chapter will explore literature in relation to prevalence of alcohol use disorders amongst young people in the criminal justice system. Secondly, it aimed to narratively review worldwide studies of the effectiveness of alcohol brief interventions in the various stages of the criminal justice system for young people aged up to 18.

Methods

We carried out a review of the international literature using the Preferred Reporting Items for Systematic reviews and Meta-Analyses (PRISMA) guidelines, which ensure comprehensive reporting within systematic reviews (39). This systematic review was conducted using the same methods to our previous reviews (40, 41).

Searches

The following databases, EBSCO (Child Development & Adolescent Studies, CINAHL Complete, Criminal Justice Abstracts with Full Text, MEDLINE, APA PsycArticles, Psychology and Behavioral Sciences Collection, APA PsycInfo) and Scopus, were searched using the search terms alcohol, screening, crime, police probation, court, jail, prison and variations of these in the title, keywords and abstract. Any language article was eligible for inclusion, but articles predating 2000 were not considered, and searches were restricted to 2000–present (January 2022). We only included articles where alcohol prevalence could be extracted.

Two authors were involved in the sifting of the published articles. Endnote was used to manage the data in the sifting stages, whilst data extraction was carried out using Microsoft Excel. Data was extracted in the same way as our previous review, using the same data extraction tables, except that the country of study was added to the prevalence extraction table (41).

Grey literature was also searched from around the world, with variations of the search terms being entered into Google and the first 300 hits were investigated. We also interrogated our previous articles on the subject (41, 42), screened the reference lists of included articles and reached out through the International Network on Brief Interventions for Alcohol & Other Drugs (INEBRIA – http:// inebria.net/) and Twitter to obtain any further articles, and to ensure no potentially relevant studies had been overlooked.

The aim was to identify the prevalence of alcohol use disorders and brief alcohol interventions in the criminal justice system worldwide for young people aged 18 and under, by searching the available evidence.

Inclusion criteria

Any language article worldwide was eligible for inclusion. Articles were included in the review if they contained information around alcohol use prevalence or were trials investigating the efficacy of alcohol brief interventions for young people aged 18 and under, within the criminal justice system. The following criteria were used for selection.

(i) Alcohol Use Prevalence

This review sought to identify the prevalence of alcohol use disorders in the criminal justice system worldwide, we included studies that mentioned daily alcohol use or use of any of the following tools.

AUDIT

The Alcohol Use Disorders Identification Test (AUDIT) is considered to be the gold standard of tools used to identify alcohol use disorder in healthcare settings (43). The AUDIT enables prevalence scores and is not a diagnostic tool.

The ten-question AUDIT is scored between 0 and 40. A score of 8+ for adults okindicates an alcohol use disorder, 8–15 indicates hazardous drinking, 16–19 harmful drinking and a score of 20+ indicates probable dependence (44). It has been shown to have 92% sensitivity and 94% specificity (44). Furthermore, it has been shown to be effective in the various stages of the criminal justice system (45). For young people, optimal scores for identifying likely alcohol use disorders using the ten-question AUDIT range from 2 to 10 (46). Across a 14- to 18-year-old age range, likely hazardous or harmful drinking has been identified at an AUDIT score of 2+ and probable dependent drinking at an AUDIT score of 3+ with sensitivity and specificity values of 83 and 93%, respectively (47).

AUDIT-C

It is also possible to use the first three questions of the AUDIT (AUDIT-C) where it has been found that a score of ≥ 3 was the optimal cut-off point for at-risk drinking (sensitivity 0.89, 95% CI 0.89–0.91; specificity 0.97, 95% CI 0.96–0.97), monthly episodic alcohol use (sensitivity 0.76, 95% CI 0.73–0.80; specificity 0.98, 95% CI 0.97–0.98) and alcohol abuse (sensitivity 0.91, 95% CI 0.85–0.95; specificity 0.90, 95% CI 0.88–0.91) (12).

RCQ-A

The Risks and Consequences Questionnaire (RCQ) measures the problems associated with alcohol and marijuana use (missing school, relationship difficulty, etc.). At baseline it covers 12 months pre-incarceration and at 3 months after release. It covers 90 days post-incarceration. Alcohol (RCQ-A) and marijuana (RCQ-M) scales (11 items, each) are scored according to whether events occurred (yes/no). It is reliable and valid for use with incarcerated adolescents, with Cronbach's alpha ranging from 0.72 to 0.83 (48).

CRAFFT

The CRAFFT (Car, Relax, Alone, Forget, Family/Friends and Trouble) tool is a six-question tool (47). A score of 2+ is indicative of a positive screen and has been validated as a measure of at-risk substance use behaviours (47, 49).

(ii) Alcohol Brief Interventions

Using the same literature searches we also looked to include trials of alcohol brief interventions in the criminal justice system around the world related to young people. We included studies that included psychosocial interventions up to a total of three hours of alcohol brief interventions either in one or multiple sessions. We only included studies if we were able to retrieve data related to young people aged up to 18.

TIDieR

We used the Template for Intervention Description and Replication (TIDieR) checklist to ascertain how interventions are reported in the included studies (50).

Quality Assessment (QA)

The relevant screening tools from the Critical Appraisal Skills Programme (CASP) were used to quality assess any included articles (51). The QA was carried out across members of the authors research team with 20% being double checked. High risk of bias was recorded if 'no' or 'unsure' was recorded for 6 or more of the 11 questions on the tool. Medium risk of bias was assigned if 'no' or 'unsure' was recorded for 4–5 questions and low risk for 1–3 questions, as in our previous study (42).

Results

In total 10,898 articles were identified from the initial searches. Following the first sift, 189 full articles were assessed for inclusion. After the completion of the full text screening, six articles were deemed eligible for inclusion in the final analysis (21, 52–56). Figure 6.1 provides a breakdown of the numbers of articles and grey literature excluded at each stage.

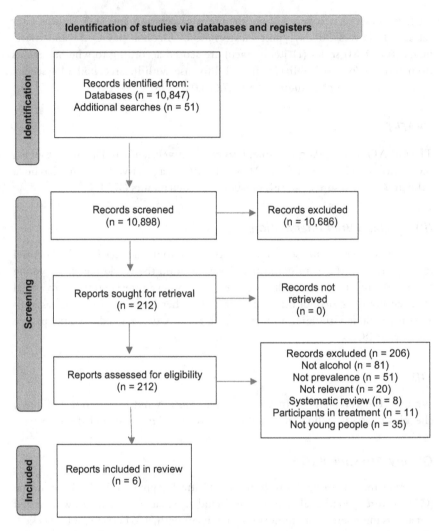

FIGURE 6.1 Data flow

Quality assessment

All six studies were identified as having a low risk of bias (Table 6.1).

Prevalence of alcohol use disorders

Study 1: Thayer et al. used the AUDIT screening tool with a cut-off score of 4 with young people in the criminal justice system in the USA and found that 59% of the population were positive for an alcohol use disorder. No information was given on dependency (56). (Table 6.2)

TABLE 6.1 Quality assessment

Author (year)	Quality assessment
Freudenberg et al. (52)	Low risk
Yurasek et al. (53)	Low risk
Stein, Clair et al., (54)	Low risk
Stein, Lebeaue et al., (55)	Low risk
Thayer et al. (56)	Low risk
Newbury-Birch et al. (21)	Low risk

Study 2/3: Newbury-Birch et al. used cut-offs for adults and young people in prison and youth offending teams in England (21). When they used adult cut-offs on AUDIT, they found that 64% had an alcohol use disorder (8+ on AUDIT) with 30% scoring positive for probably dependency (20+ on AUDIT). When using the cut-offs proposed by Knight et al. (47) for young people, they found that 81+ scored positive for an alcohol use disorder (2+) on AUDIT whilst the majority (77%) scored positive for probable dependency.

Study 4: A study was carried out in the USA of health and social characteristics of people leaving New York City Jails was carried out by Freudenberg et al. (52). They included 706 male adolescents (aged 16–18) and included a question relating to daily alcohol use. Of the included adolescents 34% reported daily drinking (52).

Study 5: Yurasek et al. identified the levels of substance use amongst 348 young people in a family court intake process and found that 56% scored positive for an alcohol use disorder using the CRAFFT tool (53).

Efficacy/effectiveness of interventions

Two slightly different result articles were carried out from one study (Table 6.3) (54, 55).

Study 1: Stein, Clair et al. (54)

Stein, Clair et al reported on 189 adolescents were randomly assigned to receive motivational interviewing or Relaxation Training. At the three-month follow-up assessment they found that motivational interviewing reduced the risk associated with marijuana. Although there was a trend towards reducing risks associated with alcohol, this was not significant (54).

Study 2: Stein, Lebeaue et al. (55)

Stein, Lebeaue et al. used the same study as Stein, Clair et al. (54), however, only included 162 adolescents. Again, although there was a trend towards reducing risks associated with alcohol, this was not significant (55) (Table 6.4).

TABLE 6.2 Alcohol use disorder prevalence

Young people

Author (year)	Country	% m/f (total n)	Age	Tool used	Alcohol use disorder positive	Alcohol use disorder ranges
Thayer et al. (56)	USA	80% male (n = 125)	16.6 ± 1.1	AUDIT	59% (4+)	None given
Freudenberg et al. (52)	USA	100% male (n = 706)	17.3 ± 0.79	Daily alcohol	34%	None given
Yurasek et al. (53)	USA	67% male (n = 348)	15.7 ± 1.27	CRAFFT	56%	
Newbury-Birch et al. (21)	England	85% male YOT/prison (n = 411)	11–17	AUDIT	64% (8+)	Haz = 22%; Harm = 12%; PD = 30%
Newbury-Birch et al. (21)	England	85% male YOT/prison (n = 411)	11–17	AUDIT	81% (2+)	PD = 77%

Notes: Haz, hazardous drinking; Harm, harmful drinking; PD, probably depended; LR, low risk of bias; RCQ-A.

TABLE 6.3 Details of included articles of efficacy studies of alcohol brief interventions in the criminal justice system for young people

Stein, Clair et al. (USA) (54)	Mean 17.1 ± 1.1 (33% White; 29% Hispanic; 28% African American) [86% male] (*n* = 189)	3 months (86%)	Risk and Consequences Questionnaire- Alcohol (Researcher)	Two sessions of MI (1 = 90 mins; 2 = 60 mins) [*n* = 189 randomised, no breakdown given]	Two sessions of relaxation training (1 = 90 mins; 2 = 60 mins)
Stein, Lebeau et al. (USA) (55)	Mean 17.1 ± 1.1(32% Hispanic; 30% African American; 30% White) [84% male] (*n* = 162)				

MI, motivational interviewing; mins, minutes; TAU, treatment as usual.

TABLE 6.4 Outcome measures and significant results of included studies

Author	Outcomes (measures)	Significant results
Stein, Clair et al. (54)	Risk and consequences of drinking (RCQ-A) Depression (CES-D)	No significant results related to alcohol.
Stein, Lebeau et al. (55)	Alcohol and drug use (structured clinical interview for DSM-IV) Depression (CES-D) Alcohol use (TLFB)	No significant results related to alcohol.

RCQ-A, Risks and Consequence Questionnaire – Alcohol; CES-D, Centre for Epidemiological Studies – Depression; TLFB, Time-Line Follow Back.

Table 6.5 shows the results in relation to details of the components involved in the Stein studies using the TIDieR tool (50).

Discussion

We carried out a systematic review of the international literature used in Chapters 3, 6 and analysed data relating to young people. Within this chapter, we included five articles from four studies in relation to prevalence of alcohol use disorders (21, 52, 53, 56) and two articles from one study in relation to efficacy (54, 55). The included studies were from the UK and the USA.

We found high levels of alcohol use disorders ranging from 34% and levels of dependence (only in the UK) at 30% using adult cut-offs and 77% using adolescent cut-offs. We found no evidence of efficacy for alcohol brief interventions in the one study included.

There is no doubt that more studies are needed for young people in relation to the prevalence of alcohol use disorders and efficacy studies in relation to alcohol screening and brief intervention in the criminal justice system worldwide. We found that studies included both alcohol and drug use in their prevalence and efficacy studies meaning we could not disentangle literature related to alcohol and the authors who carry out these studies need to report these separately. Furthermore, we found that "ever drank" was used a lot as a mechanism for reporting alcohol use which is not a good proxy or an alcohol use disorder.

As in other chapters, one of the problems in relation to studies in this setting is studies using different measurement tools and outcomes, with outcomes decided upon based on the research funding. We have recently published a Core Outcome Set for Alcohol Brief Interventions to improve the measurement of alcohol-related change (57–59) which will help researchers use the same measurements in studies of brief interventions in the future.

We have argued elsewhere that academics need to spend more time working with the criminal justice system to understand processes and be able to advise on what tools to use and how studies can best help the evidence based (60).

TABLE 6.5 TIDieR results of included brief intervention studies for Stein, Clair et al. (54) and Stein, Lebeaue et al. (55)

Provide the name or a phrase that describes the intervention.	MI
Describe any rationale, theory or goal of the elements essential to the intervention.	MI based on work of Miller & Rollnick (58).
For each category of intervention provider, describe their expertise, background and any specific training given.	Research counsellors delivered both type of intervention. Treatments were manualised and 20 hours training was given as well as weekly supervision.
Describe the mode of delivery of the intervention and whether it was provided individually or in a group.	One on one sessions.
Describe the number of times the intervention was delivered and over what period of time including the number of sessions, their schedule, and their duration, intensity or dose.	One 90-minute session and one 60 minutes booster session.
If the intervention was planned to be personalised, titrated or adapted, then describe what, why, when and how. Planned: if intervention adherence of fidelity was assessed, describe how and by whom, and if any strategies were used to maintain or improve fidelity, describe them.	MI: personalised intervention. RT: personalised as individual described relaxing place – individual to them. Adolescents and research counsellors completed evaluation forms assessing whether core components of the interventions occurred.
Actual: describe the extent to which the intervention was delivered as planned.	

Chapter summary

We carried out a systematic review of the international literature in relation to alcohol use disorders and efficacy of interventions and found very little literature in relation to young people in the criminal justice system.

In the few studies we included, we found high levels of alcohol use disorders amongst the included studies and no evidence of efficacy for brief alcohol interventions. We need more studies across the world in the field using recognised tools.

References

1. Graham L, Parkes T, McAuley A, Doi L. Alcohol problems in the criminal justice system: An opportunity for intervention. Denmark: World Health Organization Regional Office for Europe; 2012.

2. Odgers CL, Caspi A, Nagin DS, Piquero AR, Slutske WS, Milne BJ, et al. Is it important to prevent early exposure to drugs and alcohol among adolescents? Psychological Science. 2008;19(10):1037–44.

3. Giles E, McGeechan G, Coulton S, Deluca P, Drummond C, Howel D, et al. Brief alcohol intervention for risky drinking in young people aged 14 15 years in secondary schools: the SIPS JR-HIGH RCT. London: Public Health Research; 2019.

4. Battistella G, Fornari E, Annoni JM, Chtioui H, Dao K, Fabritius M, et al. Long-term effects of cannabis on brain structure. Neuropsychopharmacology. 2014;39(9):2041–8.

5. Copeland WE, Adair CE, Smetanin P, Stiff D, Briante C, Colman I, et al. Diagnostic transitions from childhood to adolescence to early adulthood. Journal of Child Psychology and Psychiatry. 2013;54(7):791–9.

6. Parlar M, MacKillop E, Petker T, Murphy J, MacKillop J. Cannabis use, age of initiation, and neurocognitive performance: Findings from a large sample of heavy drinking emerging adults. Journal of the International Neuropsychological Society. 2021;27(6):533–45.

7. Digital NHS. Smoking, drinking and drug use among young people in England in 2016. Leeds: NHS Digital; 2017.

8. Department for Education. Permanent and Fixed-period Exclusions in England: 2015 to 2016. London: Department for Education; 2017.

9. Aldington S, Harwood M, Cox B, Weatherall M, Beckert L, Hansell A, et al. Cannabis use and risk of lung cancer: A case-control study. European Respiratory Journal. 2008;31(2):280–6.

10. World Health Organization. Global status report on alcohol and health, 2014. Geneva: WHO; 2014.

11. Digital NHS. Smoking, drinking and drug use among young people. Leeds: NHS Digital; 2018.

12. Deluca P, Coulton S, Alam M, Boniface S, Donoghue K, Gilvarry E, et al. Adolescent alcohol use disorders presenting through emergency departments: Development and randomised controlled trial of age-specific alcohol screening and brief interventions (SIPS Junior Research Programme). London: NIHR Journals Library; 2020.

13. Kaner E, Bland M, Cassidy P, Coulton S, Dale V, Deluca P, et al. Effectiveness of screening and brief alcohol intervention in primary care (SIPS trial): pragmatic cluster randomised controlled trial. BMJ. 2013;346:e8501 doi: 10.1136/bmj.e8501

14. Drummond C, Deluca P, Coulton S, Bland M, Cassidy P, Crawford M, et al. The effectiveness of alcohol screening and brief intervention in emergency departments: A multicentre pragmatic cluster randomized controlled trial. PLoS One. 2014;9(6):e99463.

15. Newbury-Birch D, Coulton S, Bland M, Cassidy P, Dale V, Deluca P, et al. Alcohol screening and brief interventions for offenders in the probation setting (SIPS Trial): A pragmatic multicentre cluster randomised controlled trial. Alcohol and Alcoholism. 2014;49(5):540–8.

16. Newbury-Birch D, Scott S, O'Donnell A, Coulton S, Howel D, McColl E, et al. A pilot feasibility cluster randomised controlled trial of screening and brief alcohol intervention to prevent hazardous drinking in young people aged 14–15 in a high school setting (SIPS JR-HIGH). London: NIHR Public Health Research Program Report; 2014.

17. Williams R, Vinson DC. Validation of a single screening question for problem drinking. Journal of Family Practice. 2001;50(4):307–12.

18. Coulton S, Giles EL, McGeechan GJ, Deluca P, Drummond C, Howel D, et al. The effectiveness and cost-effectiveness of screening and brief alcohol intervention to reduce alcohol consumption in young people in the high school setting: A pragmatic randomized controlled trial (SIPS JR-HIGH). Alcohol and Alcoholism. 2022;57(2):261–9.

19. Boden J, Fergusson D, Horwood L. Alcohol misuse and violent behavior: Findings from a 30-year longitudinal study. Drug & Alcohol Dependence. 2012;122(1–2):135–41.

20. Richardson A, Budd T. Alcohol, crime and disorder: a study of young adults. Report No.: Home Office Research Study 263. London: Home Office Research, Development and Statistics Directorate; 2003 February.

21. Newbury-Birch D, Jackson K, Hodgson T, Gilvarry E, Cassidy P, Coulton S, et al. Alcohol-related risk and harm amongst young offenders aged 11–17. International Journal of Prisoner Health. 2015;11(2):75–86.

22. Gyateng T, Moretti A, May T, Turnbull P. Young people and the secure estate: Needs and interventions. Institute for Criminal Policy Research. London: Youth Justice Board; 2014.

23. Wilson E. Youth justice interventions – Findings from the juvenile cohort study (JCS). London: Ministry of Justice Analytical Series; 2013.

24. Coulton S, Nizalova O, Pellatt-Higgins T, Stevens A, Hendrie N, Marchand C, et al. RISKIT-CJS: Pragmatic randomized controlled trial to evaluate the effectiveness and cost-effectiveness of a multi-component intervention to reduce substance use and risk-taking behaviour in adolescents involved in the criminal justice system 14/183/02. London: NIHR PHR; in press.

25. Coulton S, Stockdale K, Marchand C, Hendrie N, Billings J, Boniface S, et al. Pragmatic randomised controlled trial to evaluate the effectiveness and cost effectiveness of a multi-component intervention to reduce substance use and risk-taking behaviour in adolescents involved in the criminal justice system: A trial protocol (RISKIT-CJS). BMC Public Health. 2017;17(1):246 https://doi.org/10.1186/s12889-017-4170-6

26. Newbury-Birch D, Jackson K, Hodgson T, Gilvarry E, Cassidy P, Coulton S, et al. Alcohol-related risk and harm amongst young offenders aged 11–17. International Journal of Prisoner Health. 2015;11(2):75–86.

27. Youth Justice Board/Ministry of Justice Statistics Bulletin. Youth justice statistics 2013/14. England and Wales. Newport: Office for National Statistics; 2015.

28. Unit SE. Reducing reoffending by ex-prisoners. London: Bristol University; 2002. www.bristol.ac.uk/poverty/downloads/keyofficialdocuments/Reducing%20Reoffending.pdf

29. Newbury-Birch D, Gilvarry E, McArdle P, Stewart S, Walker J, Lock C, et al. The impact of alcohol consumption on young people: A review of reviews. London: Department of Children Schools and Families; 2009.

30. Coffey C, Veit F, Wolfe R, Cini E, Patton GC. Mortality in young offenders: Retrospective cohort study. BMJ. 2003;326(7398):1064.

31. Galahad SMS Ltd. Substance misuse and juvenile offenders. London: Youth Justice Board; 2004.

32. Ritakallio M, Kaltiala-Heino R, Kivivuori J, Rimpela M. Delinquent behaviour and depression in middle adolescence: A Finnish community sample. Journal of Adolescence. 2005;28:155–9.

33. Galahad SMS Ltd. Evaluation of the substance misuse project in the young person's secure estate. London: Youth Justice Board; 2009.

34. Bardone A, Moffitt T, Caspi A, Dickson N, Stanton W, Silva P. Adult physical health outcomes of adolescent girls with conduct disorder, depression and anxiety. Journal of the American Academy of Child and Adolescent Psychiatry. 1998;37(6):594–601.

35. Willmott D, van Olphen J. Challenging the health impacts of incarceration: The role for community health workers. Californian Journal of Health Promotion. 2005;3(2):38–48.

36. British Medical Association. Young lives behind bars: the health and human rights of children and young people detained in the criminal justice system. London: British Medical Association; 2014.

37. Anderson L, Vostanis P, Spencer N. Health needs of young offenders. Journal of Child Health Care. 2004;8(2):149–64.

38. Stallard P, Thomason J, Churchyard S. The mental health of young people attending a Youth Offending Team: A descriptive study. Journal of Adolescence. 2003;26(1):33–43.

39. Rethlefsen ML, Kirtley S, Waffenschmidt S, Ayala AP, Moher D, Page MJ, et al. PRISMA-S: An extension to the PRISMA statement for reporting literature searches in systematic reviews. Systematic Reviews. 2021;10(1):39.

40. Newbury-Birch D, Ferguson J, Connor N, Divers A, Waller G. A rapid systematic review of worldwide alcohol use disorders and brief alcohol interventions in the criminal justice system. Frontiers in Psychiatry-Addictive Disorders. 2022;13:900186. doi: 10.3389/fpsyt.2022.900186

41. Newbury-Birch D, McGovern R, Birch J, O'Neill G, Kaner H, Sondhi A, et al. A rapid systematic review of what we know about alcohol use disorders and brief interventions in the criminal justice system. International Journal of Prisoner Health. 2016;12(1):57–70.

42. Newbury-Birch D, Ferguson J, Landale S, Giles EL, McGeechan GJ, Gill C, et al. A systematic review of the efficacy of alcohol interventions for incarcerated people. Alcohol and Alcoholism. 2018;53(4):412–25.

43. Hodgson R, Alwyn T, John B, Thom B, Smith A. The FAST alcohol screening test. Alcohol and Alcoholism. 2002;37(1):61–6.

44. Saunders JB, Aasland OG, Babor TF, De La Fuente JR, Grant M. Development of the Alcohol Use Disorders Identification Test (AUDIT): WHO collaborative project on early detection of persons with harmful alcohol consumption. Addiction. 1993;88(6):791–804.

45. Coulton S, Newbury-Birch D, Cassidy P, Dale V, Deluca P, Gilvarry E, et al. Screening for alcohol use in criminal justice settings: An exploratory study. Alcohol and Alcoholism. 2012;47(4):423–7.

46. Clark D, Moss H. Providing alcohol-related screening and brief interventions to adolescents through health care systems: Obstacles and solutions. PLoS Medicine. 2010;7(3): e1000214. https://doi.org/10.1371/journal.pmed.1000214

47. Knight JR, Sherritt L, Harris SK, Gates EC, Chang G. Validity of brief alcohol screening tests among adolescents: A comparison of the AUDIT, POSIT, CAGE, and CRAFFT. Alcoholism: Clinical and Experimental Research. 2003;27(1):67–73.

48. Stein L, Colby S, Barnett N, Monti P, Golembeske C, Lebeau-Craven R. Effects of motivational interviewing for incarcerated adolescents on driving under the influence after release. American Journal on Addictions. 2006;15:50–7.

49. Dhalla S, Zumbo BD, Poole G. A review of the psychometric properties of the CRAFFT instrument: 1999–2010. Current Drug Abuse Reviews. 2011;4(1):57–64.

50. Hoffman T, Glasziou P, Boutron I, Milne R, Perera R, Moher D, et al. Better reporting of interventions: Template for intervention description and replication (TIDieR) checklist and guide. BMJ. 2014;348:g1687.

51. CASP-UK. Critical Appraisal Skills Programme (CASP). London, Oxford; 2002. https://casp-uk.net

52. Freudenberg N, Daniels J, Crum M, Perkins T, Richie BE. Coming home from jail: the social and health consequences of community reentry for women, male adolescents, and their families and communities. American Journal of Public Health. 2005;95(10):1725–36.

53. Yurasek AM, Kemp K, Otero J, Tolou-Shams M. Substance use screening and rates of treatment referral among justice-involved youth. Addictive Behaviors. 2021;122:107036.

54. Stein L, Clair M, Lebeau R, Colby S, Barnett N, Golembeske C, et al. Motivational interviewing to reduce substance-related consequences: Effects for incarcerated adolescents with depressed mood. Drug and Alcohol Dependence. 2011;118(2–3):475–8.

55. Stein L, Lebeau R, Colby S, Barnett N, Golembeske C, Monti P. Motivational interviewing for incarcerated adolescents: Effects of depressive symptoms on reducing alcohol and marijuana use after release. Journal of Studies on Alcohol and Drugs. 2011;72(3):497–506.

56. Thayer RE, Callahan TJ, Weiland BJ, Hutchison KE, Bryan AD. Associations between fractional anisotropy and problematic alcohol use in juvenile justice-involved adolescents. American Journal of Drug and Alcohol Abuse. 2013;39(6):365–71.

57. Shorter G, Heather N, Bray J, Giles E, Holloway A, Barbosa C, et al. The 'Outcome Reporting in Brief Intervention Trials: Alcohol' (ORBITAL) framework: Protocol to determine a core outcome set for efficacy and effectiveness trials of alcohol screening and brief intervention. Trials. 2018;18(1):611.

58. Shorter GW, Bray JW, Giles EL, O'donnell AJ, Berman AH, Holloway A, et al. The variability of outcomes used in efficacy and effectiveness trials of alcohol brief interventions: A systematic review. Journal of Studies on Alcohol and Drugs. 2019;80(3):286–98.

59. Shorter GW, Heather N, Bray JW, Berman AH, Giles EL, O'Donnell AJ, et al. Prioritization of outcomes in efficacy and effectiveness of alcohol brief intervention trials: International multi-stakeholder e-delphi consensus study to inform a core outcome set. Journal of Studies on Alcohol and Drugs. 2019;80(3):299–309.

60. Newbury-Birch D, McGeechan G, Holloway A. Climbing down the steps from the ivory tower: How UK academics and practitioners need to work together on alcohol studies (Editorial). International Journal of Prisoner Health. 2016;12(3):129–34.

7

THE EFFICACY OF PSYCHOSOCIAL BRIEF ALCOHOL INTERVENTIONS FOR RISKY DRINKERS IN THE CRIMINAL JUSTICE SYSTEM

Introduction

As shown in previous chapters, levels of alcohol use disorders and probable dependence is high across all areas of the criminal justice system. The aim of this systematic review was to systematically review the international literature on the efficacy or effectiveness of alcohol screening and brief alcohol interventions for individuals involved in the criminal justice system on either consumption of alcohol or other social outcomes. This information will enable us to ascertain evidence-based interventions.

We included studies with control groups comprising of treatment as usual, information-only, assessment only, no assessment or another intervention. Studies eligible for this review were peer-reviewed trials of any alcohol brief interventions carried out in any setting within any area of the criminal justice system. We included interventions that were categorised as brief interventions as well as extended longer alcohol psychosocial interventions (extended brief interventions) of three hours or less. We included individuals aged 16 years or over and any outcome measure. We excluded studies that included a drug and alcohol intervention where alcohol information could not be isolated.

We carried out a review of the international literature, using the Preferred Reporting Items for Systematic reviews and Meta-Analyses (PRISMA) guidelines, which ensure comprehensive reporting within systematic reviews (1). This systematic review was conducted using the same methods to our previous reviews (2, 3).

Searches

The following databases, EBSCO (Child Development & Adolescent Studies, CINAHL Complete, Criminal Justice Abstracts with Full Text, MEDLINE,

DOI: 10.4324/9781003169802-7

APA PsycArticles, Psychology and Behavioral Sciences Collection, APA PsycInfo) and Scopus, were searched using the search terms alcohol, screening, crime, police probation, court, jail, prison and variations of these in the title, keywords and abstract. Any language article was eligible for inclusion, but articles predating 2000 were not considered, and searches were restricted to 2000–January 2022. We only included articles where alcohol prevalence could be extracted.

Two authors were involved in the sifting of the published articles. Endnote was used to manage the data in the sifting stages, whilst data extraction was carried out using Microsoft Excel. Data was extracted in the same way as our previous review, using the same data extraction tables, except that the country of study was added to the prevalence extraction table (3).

Grey literature was also searched from around the world, with variations of the search terms being entered into Google and the first 300 hits were investigated. We also interrogated our previous articles on the subject (3, 4), screened the reference lists of included articles and reached out through the International Network on Brief Interventions for Alcohol & Other Drugs (INEBRIA – http://inebria.net/) and Twitter to obtain any further articles, and to ensure no potentially relevant studies had been overlooked.

Quality assessment

The relevant screening tools from the Critical Appraisal Skills Programme (CASP) were used to quality assess any included articles (5). The quality assessment was carried out across members of the authors research team with 20% being double checked. High risk of bias was recorded if 'no' or 'unsure' was recorded for 6 or more of the 11 questions on the tool. Medium risk of bias was assigned if 'no' or 'unsure' was recorded for 4–5 questions and low risk for 1–3 questions, as in our previous study (4).

Intervention reporting

We used the Template for Intervention Description and Replication (TIDieR) check list to ascertain how interventions are reported in the included studies (6).

RESULTS

In total 10,898 articles were identified from the initial searches. Following the first sift, 189 full articles were assessed for inclusion. After the completion of the full text screening, 11 articles were deemed eligible for inclusion. Figure 7.1 provides a breakdown of the numbers of articles and grey literature excluded at each stage. Seven studies were from the UK (7–13) and four from the United States (14–17). The study populations ranged from 7 to 9,450 with 15,736 individuals in included studies. The majority of participants were male (Table 7.1).

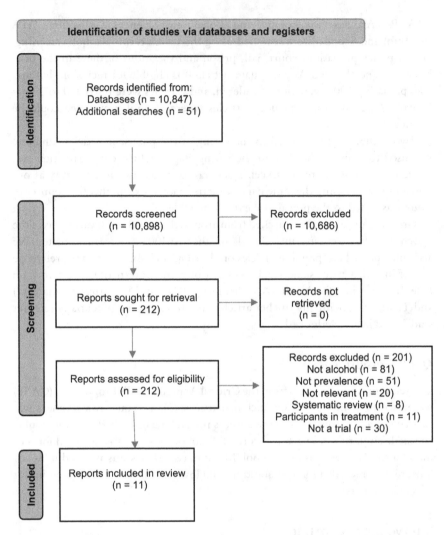

FIGURE 7.1 Data flow

In terms of screening for alcohol use disorders, most studies ($n = 9$) used the AUDIT screening tool (7–11, 14, 17–19). One used the FORM-90 (15) and one the ASSIST (16) (Table 7.2).

    AUDIT: The AUDIT, which is considered to be the gold standard of tools, used to identify alcohol use disorders in healthcare settings (20). The ten-question AUDIT is scored between 0 and 40. A score of 8+ for adults indicates an alcohol use disorder, 8–15 indicates hazardous drinking, 16–19 harmful drinking and a score of 20+ indicates probable dependence (21). It has been shown to have 92% sensitivity and 94% specificity (21).

Furthermore, it has been shown to be effective in the various stages of the criminal justice system (22).

FORM-90: The Form-90 measures quantity and frequency of alcohol use in the 30 days previous; and a checklist with *Diagnostic and Statistical Manual of Mental Disorders, 4th Edition* (DSM-IV) SUD criteria (23).

WHO-ASSIST: The ASSIST is an instrument developed by the World Health Organization (WHO) to screen for hazardous, harmful and dependent use of tobacco, alcohol and drugs (nonmedical use). The ASSIST has high internal consistency across drugs examined (0.77–0.94) and acceptable correlations between ASSIST scores and measures of risk factors for alcohol and drug use problems (0.48–0.76) (24). Following ASSIST administration, separate risk scores for each drug are calculated, with scores falling within a low-, moderate-, or high-risk range (24).

Custody suite setting

Four studies from the UK were found in relation to the custody suite (7–10). Two of the studies were from different phases of the same study (8, 9).

Study 1: A small study of motivation interviewing and brief intervention ($n = 12$) was carried out, however, no information was given on what the intervention involved. All participants were followed up at 12 weeks (7). No differences were found between groups.

Study 2 and 3: A study (carried out in two phases) to deliver alcohol screening and brief interventions between 2007 and 2010 (of less than 30 minutes each) was carried out in either custody suites or a non-custodial setting with 12 police forces across the UK. They used matched control groups with the main outcome being difference in number of arrests between both groups (8, 9). No differences were found between groups.

Study 4: Addison et al. (2018) carried out a pilot feasibility study of brief interventions in police custody suites and compared two interventions (1: 10 minutes of brief advice; 2: 10 minutes of brief advice as well as 20 minutes of brief alcohol counselling) to control condition of feedback and a leaflet with a 6- and 12-month follow-up period.

Magistrates court

A complex pragmatic study from the UK was found for the magistrates' court setting (12). The control group was usual care ($n = 134$) and was compared to a single short 15–20 manualised one-on-one session of brief intervention in a magistrates court in Wales, UK (19).

Although there were no significant findings found in any of the alcohol use measures (AUDIT, total number of standard weekly drinks or number of drinking days) or recidivism. Injury was significantly less for those who had received the intervention (27.4%) than those who had not [39.6%; CI = −0.23, −0.009]. At three-month follow-up, significantly more participants in the intervention group (31%; n = 37) than control group (16%; n = 18) demonstrated an increase in their readiness to change drinking behaviour (χ^2 = 8.56; df = 2; P = 0.014), but this did not persist at 12-month follow-up (19).

Probation

Two studies from the UK were found in the probation setting (11, 18).

> **Study 1:** A pragmatic cluster randomised controlled trial of the effectiveness of two different brief intervention strategies compared to a control condition of feedback on AUDIT score and an information leaflet at reducing risky drinking in the probation setting across various sites in England (North East, South East and London) was carried out by Newbury-Birch et al. (18). Probation officers were randomised to one of the three conditions – each of which built upon the previous feedback on screening outcome and a client information leaflet control group, five minutes of structured brief advice, and 20 minutes of brief lifestyle counselling. Sixty eight per cent and 60% of participants were followed up at 6 and 12 months, respectively (18). No significant differences between groups were found in relation to AUDIT status. Those in the brief advice and brief lifestyle counselling intervention groups were statistically significantly less likely to reoffend (36 and 38%, respectively) than those in the information leaflet control group (50%) in the year following intervention (18).
>
> **Study 2:** A pilot randomised controlled trial with offenders on probation on community service orders was carried out in Scotland (11). In total, 82 offenders were randomised (no information on randomisation group was given for 11 offenders). As the study only followed up 22% of participants, the study team were unable to give any effectiveness results (11).

Prison

Four studies from the United States were found for the prison system (14–17).

> *Study 1:* Begun et al. (2011) carried out a randomised controlled trial of alcohol screening and brief intervention amongst incarcerated women in the United States and followed up 2 months post release from prison. Despite intense attempts to follow up, only 20% were followed up. Although they did find a mean reduction in AUDIT score greater in intervention group (F(1,148) = 6.336, p ≤ 0.001) because of the low follow-up rates, this should be taken with caution.

TABLE 7.1 Details of included articles

Author (country)	Age (ethnicity) [% male]	Follow-up period (follow-up rates)	Alcohol screening used and cut-off used (who screened)	Intervention [number randomised]	Control [number randomised]
Police custody suites					
Tobutt & Milani (7) (England)	MIBI: mean 25 ± 3.86; BI: 32.43 ± 7.9 (75% White British, 17% Pakistani, 8% mixed race) [92% male]	12 weeks (100%)	AUDIT 8-19 (arrest referral worker)	MIBI (no information given) [n = 5] or BI (no information given) [n = 7]	Not applicable
Kennedy et al. (8) (England)	> 90% white	6 months (7%)	AUDIT 8+ (various practitioners)	Various brief interventions (20-120 mins) [n = 2,177]	Matched control group [n = 2,177]
McCracken et al. (9) (England)	93% white	12 months (100%)	AUDIT 8+ (various practitioners)	Various brief interventions (20-120 mins) [n = 4,739]]	Matched control group [n = 4,711]
Addison et al. (10) (England)	Mean 32.47 ± 10.96 (94% White British) [83%]	6 and 12 months (25%, 23%)	AUDIT 8+ (Detention Officer)	1: Structured brief advice (5 mins) [n = 165]; 2: Structured brief advice (5 mins) and brief lifestyle counselling (20 mins) [n = 61]	Client information leaflet [n = 79]
Magistrates court					
Watt et al. (12) (Wales)	I: 23.6 ± 4.7 (92.4% White; 3.8% Black; 3.8 other) [100%] C: 22.8 ± 4.6 (93.9% White; 2.3 Black; 3.8% other) [100%]	3 and 12 months (87%, 75%)	AUDIT 8+ (Researcher)	1 session of MI (15-20 mins) [n = 135]	TAU (n = 134)
Probation					
Newbury-Birch et al. (18) (England)	Mean 31.0 + 10.9 (White 76%) [85%]	6 and 12 months (68%, 60%)	AUDIT 8+ (Offender Managers)	1: Structured brief advice (5 mins) [n = 178]; 2: Structured brief advice (5 mins) and brief lifestyle counselling (20 mins) [n = 163]	Client information leaflet [n = 184]

(continued)

TABLE 7.1 Cont.

Author (country)	Age (ethnicity) [% male]	Follow-up period (follow-up rates)	Alcohol screening used and cut-off used (who screened)	Intervention [number randomised]	Control [number randomised]
Orr et al. (11) (Scotland)	18+ no other information for the RCT	6 and 12 months (13%, 7%)	AUDIT 8–19 (Community justice staff)	BI (no information) [n = 43]	Screening and feedback [n = 39]
Prison					
Begun et al. (14) (USA)	Mean 35.7 ± 8.7 (57% African American; 31% White; 6% Hispanic) [100% female]	2 months post release (20%)	AUDIT-12 8+ (researcher)	1 session of MI (60–90 mins) [n = 468]	TAU [n = 261]
Davis et al. (15) (USA)	Mean 45.7 ± 7.7 (49% Caucasian; 38% African American) [97% male]	2 months (41%)	FORM-90 alcohol tool (researcher)	1 session of MI (60 mins) [n = 36]	TAU and information on local services [n = 37]
Owens et al. (16) (USA)	Mean age 34.4 ± 9.8 (28% Hispanic; 20% Native American/Alaskan 18% Native African American; 8% Biracial/multiracial/other) [100% male]	Between 1 and 3 months (63%)	ASSIST (Researcher)	1 session of MI (50–60 mins) [n = 23]	1 session of educational videos (50–60 mins) [n = 17]
Stein et al., (17) (USA)	Mean 34.1 ± 8.9 (71% Caucasian; 19% African American; 7% Hispanic) [100% female]	1, 3 and 6 months (76%, 79%, 79%)	AUDIT 8+ (researcher)	2 sessions of MI (45–60 mins): 2nd session 1st follow-up [n = 125]	TAU [n = 120]

MI, Motivational Interviewing; mins, minutes; TAU, treatment as usual.

TABLE 7.2 Outcome measures and significant results of included studies

Author	Outcomes (measures)	Significant results
Police custody settings		
Tobutt & Milani (7)	P: Mean AUDIT score S: Illicit drug use S: Money spent on alcohol S: Number of arrests S: Arrest type	No significant results related to alcohol.
Kennedy et al. (8)	AUDIT compared to Alcohol Intervention records General Health Questionnaire Arrest data	No significant results related to alcohol.
McCracken et al. (9)	Arrest data	No significant results related to alcohol.
Addison et al. (10)	P: eligible participants P: % followed-up S: AUDIT range S: Readiness to change (RTQ) S: Quality of life (EDQ-5-L) S: Arrest data	No significant results related to alcohol.
Magistrates court		
Watt et al., (12)	AUDIT 7-day drinking diary Illicit substance use Readiness to change (RTQ) Injury Recidivism rates	Injury was significantly less for those who had received the intervention (27.4%) than those who had not [39.6%; CI = −0.23, −0.009]. At 3-month follow-up, significantly more participants in the intervention group (31%; $n = 37$) than control group (16%; $n = 18$) demonstrated an increase in their readiness to change drinking behaviour ($\chi 2 = 8.56$; df = 2; P = 0.014), but this did not persist at 12-month follow-up.
Probation		
Newbury-Birch et al. (18)	P: 8+ on AUDIT S: Quality of life (EQ-5D) S: Readiness to change (RTQ) S: Patient satisfaction S: Service use S: Recidivism rates	OR of receiving a conviction was significantly lower in the brief advice (OR = 0.50; 95% CI = 0.33−0.80) and brief lifestyle counselling (OR = 0.54; 95% CI = 0.33−0.89) groups compared with the client information leaflet group.
Orr et al. (11)	AUDIT	No significant results related to alcohol.

(continued)

TABLE 7.2 Cont.

Author	Outcomes (measures)	Significant results
Prison		
Begun et al. (14)	P: Engagement with substance abuse treatment services P: Level of reported alcohol use (AUDIT-12)	Mean reduction in AUDIT score from baseline to follow-up were greater in the intervention group (F(1,148) = 6.336, p ≤ 0.001).
Davis et al. (15)	P: Engagement with services with VA substance abuse services (TSR) S: Contact with other substance abuse services (TSR) S: substance use (Form 90) S: Consequences (SIP) S; Addiction Severity (ASI) S: Readiness to change (RTC)	Those in the IG were statistically more likely to schedule appointments at both VA services with 60 days (66.7 vs. 41%; p = 0.025).
Owens et al. (16)	Feasibility Pre-intervention motivation and confidence ratings IDPA to assess social networks ASI criminal and treatment history Alcohol and substance use FORM-90	No significant results related to alcohol.
Stein et al. (17)	Drinking diary Alcohol use disorders (AUDIT)	Intervention effects on abstinent days were statistically significant at 3 months (odds ratio = 1.96, 95% CI 1.17,3.30).

P, Primary outcome; S, Secondary outcome; IG, Intervention Group; CG, Control Group; ASI, Addiction Severity Index; RSQ-A, Risks and Consequence Questionnaire – Alcohol; TSR, Treatment Services Review; SIP, Short Inventory of Problems; DSM-IV, Diagnostic and Statistical Manual of Mental Disorders, 4th. Edition; CES-D, Centre for Epidemiological Studies – Depression; TLFB, Time Line Follow Back; AUDIT, Alcohol Use Disorders Identification Test; VA, Veterans Association; RTQ, Readiness to Change Questionnaire; EQ-5D, Euroqol Quality of Life; OR, Odds ratio.

Study 2: Davis et al. (2003) carried out a randomised controlled trial of veterans in a US county jail. Participants were recruited in the month prior to leaving jail (7). Only 41% of participants were followed up despite various attempts being made to contact people at the two-month follow-up period (15). No effectiveness was found between groups in relation to alcohol measures. However, those in the intervention group were more likely to schedule appointments at a veterans' addiction clinic following their release (67 vs 41%; p < 0.03) (15).

Study 3: Owens and McCrady (2016) carried out a pilot randomised controlled trial with adult males in a large US detention centre in which individuals who were drinking at a moderate or high level in the 12 months

TABLE 7.3 Quality assessment/risk of bias

Author (year)	Quality assessment
Police custody suites	
Addison et al. (10)	Low risk
Kennedy et al. (8)	Medium risk
Mccracken et al. (9)	Medium risk
Tobutt & Milani (7)	High risk
Magistrates court	
Watt et al. (12)	Low risk
Probation	
Newbury-Birch et al. (18)	Low risk
Orr et al. (11)	Medium risk
Prison	
Begun et al. (14)	Medium risk
Davis et al. (15)	High risk
Owens & McCrady (16)	Medium risk
Stein et al. (17)	Low risk

prior to incarceration (16). Participants were randomised to either take part in a 50–60 minutes in person motivational interviewing intervention or were asked to watch two educational videos. Participants were followed up at three months post intervention. The study team only followed up 20% of participants and were therefore unable to show any statistical differences between groups (21).

Study 4: A randomised controlled trial to evaluate brief intervention for alcohol use and risky sexual behaviour among women in a prison in the United States was carried out by Stein et al. (2010). Women were eligible for the trial if they had consumed four or more drinks on at least three occasions in the previous three months or identified as a hazardous drinker in the past year using the AUDIT and if they had recently engaged in risky sexual behaviour. The first session of motivational interviewing was delivered in prison with the second taking place approximately one to three months after leaving prison. Participants were followed up at three and six months (17). Stein et al. (2010) found that the motivational interviewing intervention effects on abstinent days was statistically significant at three months (OR = 1.96, 95% CI 1.17,3.30). Although, this effect was not maintained at six-month follow-up. There was no significant difference between participant groups for the number of drinks consumed per drinking day (25). The study suggests that brief motivational interviewing may be effective at reducing the frequency of alcohol use in the short term but further sessions could be necessary to maintain the effect in the longer term (26).

TABLE 7.4 TIDieR results of included brief intervention studies

Study	Brief name	Why?	Rationale/ elements essential to intervention	Who?	How?	When and how much?	Tailoring	How well?
	Name or phrase to describe intervention		Rationale/ goal of intervention	Intervention provider information	Modes of delivery of intervention	N intervention delivered and period including number of sessions, schedule, duration and intensity	How intervention was tailored to individual and which theories used	Planned: Intervention adherence and strategies used to maintain or improve adherence. Actual: The extent to which the intervention was delivered as planned
Police custody suites								
Tobutt & Milani (7)	MI	MI (27)		Trained alcohol workers	One on one sessions	Standard brief intervention or motivational interviewing intervention	Not modified	None given
Kennedy et al. (8)	MI	MI (27)		Trained police officers	One on one sessions	Various ranging from 20 minutes to one hour	Not modified	None given
McCracken et al. (9)				Trained police officers	One on one sessions	20–53 minutes. Intervention included elements of motivational interviewing, information giving and advice with reference to the criminal justice system.	Not modified	None given
Addison et al. (10)	MI	MI (27)		Trained detention officers or trained alcohol councillors	One on one sessions	10 minutes brief advice or 10 mins brief advice plus 20 mins brief counselling	Not modified	None given
Magistrates court								
Watt et al. (19)	MI	MI (27)		Trained researcher	One on one sessions	15–20 minutes of brief intervention	Not modified	None given

Probation

Newbury-Birch et al. (18)	SIPS MI	MI (27)	Trained probation officers and trained councillors	One on one sessions	10 minutes brief advice or 10 mins brief advice plus 20 mins brief counselling	Not modified	Recordings were taken but no information given.
Orr et al. (11)	MI	MI (27)	Trained probation officers	One on one sessions	Not given	Not modified	None given

Prison

Begun et al. (14)	MI	MI (27)	Graduate social workers trained in research protocol engaged women in initial demographic and brief screening interview.	One on one sessions	One session of 60–90 mins per person	Not modified	None given
Davis et al. (15)	Brief MI	MI (27)	Clinical Research Staff who had completed/ were completing Masters Degrees. 12 hours of training in MI. Training: didactics and observed practices and experiences and supervision provided.	One on one sessions	One session of 69 mins per person	Not modified	None given
Owens & McCrady (16)	MI	MI (27)	Advanced clinical psychology grad tutors who were trained in MI and had experience of delivering MI.	One on one sessions	One session of 50–60 mins per person	Not modified	Sessions were recorded for supervision with a certified MI trainer and to assess treatment fidelity.

(continued)

TABLE 7.4 Cont.

Study	Brief name	Why?	Who?	How?	When and how much?	Tailoring	How well?
	Name or phrase to describe intervention	Rationale/ goal of elements essential to intervention	Intervention provider information	Modes of delivery of intervention	N intervention delivered and period including number of sessions, schedule, duration and intensity	How intervention was tailored to individual and which theories used	Planned: Intervention adherence and strategies used to maintain or improve adherence. Actual: The extent to which the intervention was delivered as planned
Stein et al. (17)	MI	MI (27)	Interventionists were trained clinicians who were trained in MI.	One on one sessions	Two sessions of between 30 and 45 mins per person	Not modified	MITI was used to train and monitor the MI skills of the interventionists. The MITI allows for assessment of threshold competence for therapists and a measure of integrity of MI interventions using two global scores ("empathy," and "spirit," score range 1–7) and seven behaviour counts (e.g. 'giving information', 'MI adherent').

TIDieR results

Results relating to how interventions were described using the TIDieR checklist in Table 7.4 (6). We found that for some categories detailed information was not given in the included articles.

Quality assessment

In relation to quality assessment, we found that four studies had a low risk of bias (10, 12, 17, 18), five had a medium risk (8, 9, 11, 14, 16) and two a high risk of bias (7, 15) (Table 7.3).

Discussion

It could be argued that the stages in the criminal justice system described above are analogous to the healthcare system. Police stations are busy and chaotic very like accident and emergency departments. Probation is similar to primary care, appointments made and an emphasis on dealing with the underlying issues, whereas prison is similar to hospital wards in as much as often the person is there for a period of time (3, 4).

Within this study we round 11 studies in relation to efficacy of alcohol screening and brief interventions within various stages of the criminal justice system. Seven from the UK and four from the USA. The studies used previous tools to screen and different outcome measures to assess efficacy or effectiveness. Furthermore, unlike other studies, we assessed the components of the interventions using the TIDiER tool (6). We were pleased to find that all studies used Rollnick and Miller motivational interviewing techniques (27); however, many components were missing from the journal articles for us to ascertain similarities and differences between the studies.

As in the chapter relating to prevalence of alcohol use disorders in the criminal justice system, one of the problems in relation to studies in this setting is studies using different measurement tools and outcomes, with outcomes decided upon based on the research funding. We have recently published a Core Outcome Set for Alcohol Brief Interventions to improve the measurement of alcohol-related change (25, 28, 29) which will help researchers use the same measurements in studies of brief interventions in the future.

We found that one of the main issues in trial in the criminal justice system is following up participants because of their sometimes chaotic lifestyles (11). We found, as other studies have (3, 4), that studies examining effectiveness of risky drinking issues are still scarce. One of the problems of carrying out research in the criminal justice system is the necessity of using self-report follow-up data (3, 4, 30). Studies need to identify ways to use routinely collected data in following participants rather than self-reported data.

Furthermore, as in health settings, the lack of good evidence in the criminal justice system is because of issues such as workload and time to carry out studies (3, 18, 26, 31).

Chapter summary

This chapter follows on from previous chapters which shows high levels of alcohol use disorders and probable dependence in the criminal justice system. This chapter detailed the findings of a systematic review of the internal literature in relation to the efficacy/effectiveness of alcohol screening and brief interventions across the various stages of the criminal justice system. We included 11 articles (seven from the UK and four from USA) in the final analysis. The majority of studies ($n = 9$) used the AUDIT screening tool with one each using the FORM-90 and one the ASSIST tool.

We found no evidence of efficacy or effectiveness, however, the included studies used different tools to screen and different outcome measures across the studies meaning that it was impossible to aggregate results. There were some promising results (such as reduced reoffending), however, more studies are needed across the criminal justice system to ascertain efficacy or effectiveness using similar outcome measures.

References

1. Rethlefsen ML, Kirtley S, Waffenschmidt S, Ayala AP, Moher D, Page MJ, et al. PRISMA-S: An extension to the PRISMA statement for reporting literature searches in systematic reviews. Systematic Reviews. 2021;10(1):39.
2. Newbury-Birch D, Ferguson J, Connor N, Divers A, Waller G. A rapid systematic review of worldwide alcohol use disorders and brief alcohol interventions in the criminal justice system. Frontiers in Psychiatry-Addictive Disorders. 2022;13:900186. doi: 10.3389/fpsyt.2022.900186. PMID: 35873244; PMCID: PMC9301009
3. Newbury-Birch D, McGovern R, Birch J, O'Neill G, Kaner H, Sondhi A, et al. A rapid systematic review of what we know about alcohol use disorders and brief interventions in the criminal justice system. International Journal of Prisoner Health. 2016;12(1):57–70.
4. Newbury-Birch D, Ferguson J, Landale S, Giles EL, McGeechan GJ, Gill C, et al. A systematic review of the efficacy of alcohol interventions for incarcerated people. Alcohol and Alcoholism. 2018;53(4):412–25.
5. CASP-UK. Critical appraisal skills programme (CASP). London, Oxford; 2002. https://casp-uk.net
6. Hoffman T, Glasziou P, Boutron I, Milne R, Perera R, Moher D, et al. Better reporting of interventions: template for intervention description and replication (TIDieR) checklist and guide. BMJ. 2014;348:g1687.
7. Tobutt C, Milani R. Comparing two counselling styles for hazardous drinkers charged with alcohol-related offences in a police custody suite: Piloting motivational interviewing brief intervention or a standard brief intervention to reduce alcohol consumption. Advances in Dual Diagnosis. 2010;3(4):20–33.
8. Kennedy A, Dunbar I, Boath M, Beynon C, Duffy P, Stafford J, et al. Evaluation of alcohol arrest referral pilot schemes (Phase 1). London: Home Office; 2012.
9. McCracken K, McMurran M, Winlow S, Sassi F, McCarthy K. Evaluation of alcohol arrest referral pilot schemes (Phase 2). London: Home Office; 2012. Available from: www.gov.uk/government/uploads/system/uploads/attachment_data/file/116267/occ102.pdf

10. Addison M, McGovern R, Angus C, Becker F, Brennan A, Brown H, et al. Alcohol screening and brief intervention in police custody suites: Pilot Cluster Randomised Controlled Trial (AcCePT). Alcohol and Alcoholism. 2018;53(5):548–59.

11. Orr K, McCoard S, Canning S, McCartney P, Williams J. Delivery alcohol brief interventions in the community justice setting: Evaluation of a pilot project. Glasgow: NHS Health Scotland; 2011.

12. Watt K, Shepherd J, Newcombe R. Drunk and dangerous: A randomised controlled trial of alcohol brief intervention for violent offenders. Journal of Experimental Criminology. 2008;4(1):1–19.

13. Newbury-Birch D, Harrison B, Brown N, Kaner E. Sloshed and sentenced: A prevalence study of alcohol use disorders among offenders in the North East of England. International Journal of Prisoner Health. 2009;5(4):201–11.

14. Begun A, Rose L, LeBel T. Intervening with women in jail around alcohol and substance abuse during preparation for community reentry. Alcoholism Treatment Quarterly. 2011;29(4):453–78.

15. Davis T, Baer J, Saxon A, Kivlahan D. Brief motivational feedback improves post-incarceration treatment contact among veterans with substance use disorders. Drug and Alcohol Dependence. 2003;69: 197–203.

16. Owens M, McCrady B. A pilot study of a brief motivational intervention for incarcerated drinkers. Journal of Substance Abuse Treatment. 2016;68:1–10.

17. Stein M, Caviness C, Anderson B, Hebert M, Clarke J. A brief alcohol intervention for hazardously drinking incarcerated women. Addiction. 2010;105(3):466–75.

18. Newbury-Birch D, Coulton S, Bland M, Cassidy P, Dale V, Deluca P, et al. Alcohol screening and brief interventions for offenders in the probation setting (SIPS Trial): A pragmatic multicentre cluster randomised controlled trial. Alcohol and Alcoholism. 2014;49(5):540–8.

19. Watt K, Shepherd J, Newcombe R. Drunk and dangerous: A randomised controlled trial of alcohol brief intervention for violent offenders. Journal of Experimental Criminology. 2008;4:1–19.

20. Hodgson R, Alwyn T, John B, Thom B, Smith A. The FAST alcohol screening test. Alcohol and Alcoholism. 2002;37(1):61–6.

21. Saunders JB, Aasland OG, Babor TF, De La Fuente JR, Grant M. Development of the Alcohol Use Disorders Identification Test (AUDIT): WHO collaborative project on early detection of persons with harmful alcohol consumption. Addiction. 1993;88(6):791–804.

22. Coulton S, Newbury-Birch D, Cassidy P, Dale V, Deluca P, Gilvarry E, et al. Screening for alcohol use in criminal justice settings: An exploratory study. Alcohol and Alcoholism. 2012;47(4):423–7.

23. Miller W. A structured interview for drinking and related behaviors: Test manual. Bethesda: National Institute on Alcohol Abuse and Alcoholism; 1996.

24. Humeniuk R, Ali R, Babor TF, Farrell M, Formigoni ML, Jittiwutikarn J, et al. Validation of the alcohol, smoking and substance involvement screening test (ASSIST). Addiction. 2008;103(6):1039–47.

25. Shorter GW, Heather N, Bray JW, Berman AH, Giles EL, O'Donnell AJ, et al. Prioritization of outcomes in efficacy and effectiveness of alcohol brief intervention trials: International multi-stakeholder e-delphi consensus study to inform a core outcome set. Journal of Studies on Alcohol and Drugs. 2019;80(3):299–309.

26. Anderson P, Bendtsen P, Spak F, Reynolds J, Drummond C, Colom J, et al. Improving the delivery of brief interventions for heavy drinking in primary health care: Outcome

results of the Optimizing Delivery of Health Care Intervention (OHDIN) five-country cluster randomized factorial trial. Addiction. 2016;111(11):1935–45.

27. Rollnick S, Miller WR, Butler C. Motivational interviewing in health care: Helping patients change behavior. New York: Guilford Publication; 2008.

28. Shorter G, Heather N, Bray J, Giles E, Holloway A, Barbosa C, et al. The 'Outcome Reporting in Brief Intervention Trials: Alcohol' (ORBITAL) framework: Protocol to determine a core outcome set for efficacy and effectiveness trials of alcohol screening and brief intervention. Trials. 2018;18(1):611.

29. Shorter GW, Bray JW, Giles EL, O'donnell AJ, Berman AH, Holloway A, et al. The variability of outcomes used in efficacy and effectiveness trials of alcohol brief interventions: A systematic review. Journal of Studies on Alcohol and Drugs. 2019;80(3):286–98.

30. Shorter G, Bray J, Heather N, Berman A, Giles E, Clarke M, et al. The "Outcome Reporting in Brief Intervention Trials: Alcohol" (ORBITAL) core outcome set: International consensus on outcomes to measure in efficacy and effectiveness trials of alcohol brief interventions. Journal of Studies on Alcohol and Drugs. 2021;82(5):638–46.

31. Brown N, Newbury-Birch D, McGovern R, Phinn E, Kaner E. Alcohol screening and brief intervention in a policing context: A mixed methods feasibility study. Drug & Alcohol Review. 2010;29:647–54.

8

THE WAY FORWARD

Researchers and practitioners working in a co-productive way to produce research in the criminal justice system

We have to start this chapter, and you will have seen by reading this book, by saying that research in the criminal justice system is difficult. However, we would argue that it is possible and it is of the upmost importance, specifically in the field of public health and crime. As Professor Chris Whitty observes, 'research is of no use unless it gets to the people who need to use it'. It is recognised that developing a coordinated approach to policy and practice takes time and requires persistence from both academics and policymakers (1).

The authors have carried out a number of research projects in the various stages of the criminal justice system (2–8). They have seen that there are a lot of competing parts to the equation including experience and expertise, values and judgements, resources, policy context, habits and traditions, and the influence of pressure groups as well as research evidence (2, 4, 9–11), and for many these competing parts are hard to navigate, therefore showing the importance of working together. One of the fundamental reasons for undertaking co-production research is the ability to influence policy and practice. Not only can research provide academic benefits, such as an original contribution to the wider literature, but it can also offer wider benefits to policy. This in turn can translate into benefits for practice. Co-produced research can also be used to influence service commissioning, which in turn can bring real change in communities, with for example, access to facilities and support groups, that otherwise may not exist for individuals and their families (12).

In Jennifer Ferguson's PhD she notes:

> Having many years of experience working on large research projects was useful but on reflection being Mrs. Ferguson and asking for ethical approval from HMPPS as a PhD student felt more difficult to asking for approval in collaboration with a number of academics and Professors was

DOI: 10.4324/9781003169802-8

very different. Undertaking prison research is a challenge because prison Governors change, different Governors are more research active than others, and Government policies change, all impacting on the priorities of those you wish to work with. I even had previous experience of collecting data in a prison and having prison keys and I never expected this to make my PhD data collection more difficult. My first visit after obtaining ethical approval to the open estate was an experience and left me feeling that I was not in the right place. The aesthetics were so different. It was beautiful. Nevertheless, it was the inside that made me uneasy. The residents were free to walk around and although I had keys, there was very little need for them. Whilst my criminological mind embraced the ideology of this, my pragmatic mind went into overdrive. I did not know how I was going to find the women. I was used to asking a prison officer to simply collect them from their cell. This feeling of insecurity became very important when understanding the conversations I then went on to have with the residents.

(13, 113)

All around the world, austerity is hitting hard, and cuts to public services are becoming common place (14). With workloads being fuller there is a reluctance for practitioners and policymakers to take on extra workload when carrying out much needed research projects in the criminal justice field. However, this is a time that research is needed more than ever as we need to provide evidence-based, cost-effective treatments. We argue that by working 'WITH' practitioners from an early stage in a co-productive way we can do this (15). Whilst there are many challenges in co-producing research in the criminal justice system, when it does happen the results can be particularly illuminating (3). Between them, the researchers have over 30 years of experience in the field and both feel that they have learned more from the practitioners than from any books they have read. Moreover, it is imperative that research is completed in the context of local. In the real world of local services work programmes are vulnerable, complex, uncertain and ambiguous (VUCA) (16). This can be difficult for researchers and it can feel complex and uncertain for the researcher who was not familiar with working in this political environment. It is important that a researcher immersives themselves in the structures and learn the politics, the language and the way of working of the institution. Of course this helps those working there to learn the same from the academic setting. In Cheetham et al.'s article, they referenced a systematic review of barriers and opportunities to evidence use in English public health decision-making and highlighted the importance of local experts in providing evidence and knowledge (17). They argue, rightly, that there is a need to develop a deeper understanding of evidence requirements from the perspective of local government decision makers, given that most published studies are from the perspectives of researchers (17, 18).

Evidence-based work in the criminal justice system

As far back as 1998, Professor Lawrence Sherman advocated for 'evidence-based policing', arguing that 'police practices should be based on scientific evidence about what works best' (19). Sherman argued that rigorous and systematic scientific research should be used to and generated by the police to make both tactical and strategic decisions. However, as others have argued, this information needs to be translated into everyday decision-making (10, 19). We all agree that this is the best and correct way to carry out research; however, practitioners often want, and in fact need 'quick fix' answers to complex problems and telling them that a project may take two years or longer to complete is frustrating to them (10). It is therefore important, some would argue, imperative, to include practitioners and individuals involved in the criminal justice staff as well as individuals involved in the criminal justice system in all stages of research (11). This would mean that both academics and criminal justice staff and those involved can share experiences and learning with and from each other. This is summed up perfectly by Shepherd as evidence needing to flow through the ecosystem from generation to end user, where both push and pull are needed (20).

However, when it comes to informing policy there tends to be an over reliance on evidence from university-led, tightly controlled intervention trials which is important; however, this can lead to questions about the applicability of research in the real world (21). It is important that strategies be put into place that ensure that we utilise a co-production method of working with practitioners and, of course, service users where possible so that the findings can be implemented (4, 11). Whilst it has been argued that academics and criminal justice practitioners may be seen by many as coming from two very different places, the boundaries between them may not be as large as many believe (22), and a co-production approach where researchers and police working together could lead to real translational research (23). This is summed up perfectly by Shepherd, 2014, as evidence needing to flow through the ecosystem from generation to end-user, where both push and pull are needed (20).

As a delivery model for health, criminal justice system and social care, co-production has been described as sharing information and decision-making between providers and service users (24, 25). This way of working is increasingly used to bring together academics, policymakers and communities to produce research that is not only academically excellent but importantly has real public benefit which can be implemented in the real world (26).

In order for true co-production to take place, it is important for academics to "climb down from the ivory tower" and spend time with agencies to fully understand the agency where the work will take place (15). This was shown in the Home Office–funded Restorative Justice Trials. The study journal article discusses the intricacies of conducting research with practitioners and mentions: "Magistrates' court clerks were not so cooperative. While two small randomised controlled trials in Northumbrian Magistrates' Courts were eventually completed, their samples were only achieved by dogged persistence of the Northumbria Manager, Dorothy Newbury-Birch" which sums up the difficulties in one sentence (27). So, how do we manage to do research effectively? In projects we have worked on, recruiting participants is not the difficult part however following them up for research projects (especially randomised controlled trials) is difficult (2, 27, 28). Often the individuals are happy to be followed up and are keen to be involved, however, often because of their chaotic lifestyles this is difficult to do (2, 4) but is expensive to do properly.

The key strength of co-production research, and aspirations of co-production researchers, is that their research has real-world application, and is picked up and used by those who would most benefit from it (15). Making a positive change for the lives of individuals, groups and communities is fundamental, particularly from a public health co-production perspective (29).

What is co-production in research?

Co-producing research is now becoming more and more prevalent around the world. It is often called different things (30). These include participatory action research (31), knowledge translation (32) and collaborative research (33). Methodology can vary greatly depending on where the research is carried out and by whom.

Many co-production projects adhere to very similar principles where the exchange, synthesis and dissemination of knowledge between researchers, policymakers, practitioners and end users is imperative (34) with a knowledge to action framework being developed.

In the book *Beyond two communities: the co-production of research, policy and practice in collaborative public health settings* (35), it is shown that getting research into practice can take up to 17 years.

In terms of approaches to co-production four distinct approaches have been identified.

1. Boundary organisations
2. Hybrid management
3. Front and back stage regions
4. Communities of practice

> **Boundary organisations**: This theoretical approach to co-production work draws on a sociopolitical perspective of boundary work and political approaches to agent theory. A unique component of boundary organisations within the wider literature on co-production is that each partner continues to negotiate the different social worlds in which they operate, however they remain accountable to their host organisation only. As such, whilst there will be a degree of compromise and commonality on the goals of the co-production work being undertaken,

each partner will retain the pressures, and competing priorities of their own organisation, whilst trying to satisfy the needs of the project (36).

Hybrid management is an adaption of boundary organisation approach, which moved away from the sociopolitical foundations of boundary organisations, instead focussing on the practices within an academic and policymaking partnership (37). Whilst within a boundary organisation approach each party retains a large degree of autonomy from one another, with a hybrid management approach partners are sufficiently intertwined so as to remove the possibility for autonomy. Four key processes are identified to facilitate hybrid management. Firstly, there needs to be a sufficient level of integration between academic and practice elements of the project, this is to ensure that they are speaking the same language (hybridisation). However, it is also essential to deconstruct these elements so that any underlying assumptions can be addressed (deconstruction). However, whilst autonomy should be impossible due to integration between academic and practice partners, there should still be clearly defined boundaries (boundary work) so that each partner knows which aspects of the project they are responsible for (cross-domain orchestration) (37).

Front stage and back stage regions looks at the distinction between how co-production work is presented to front stage and back stage audiences (38). The front stage is defined as those not directly involved in the project, such as members of the public or interested stakeholders, whilst those in the backstage are those partners directly involved in the project. According to this theory, there is a distinct difference between the messages portrayed to each audience, the front stage audience receive a performance which suggests that the project embodies certain standards. The back stage on the other hand is reserved for insiders involved in the project, where the 'performance' is deliberately contradicted (38).

Communities of practice deviates slightly from the other approaches (39). Within this approach, partners come together because they share a passion about a particular topic, and whilst they come from different backgrounds they are able to draw on their collective strengths to deepen their individual knowledge, and achieve the project aims (39).

Jennifer Ferguson, in her doctoral thesis notes:

It was very difficult for someone like me who is used to being questioned about the science of brief interventions and therefore needed to give more consideration to the culture in the women's prison. The practitioners were very rightly more concerned with the process and with the possible impact on the women. The two hours I was grilled for (very early on in my PhD) ended up being the most useful two hours of my research. When I left that room, I was deflated and exhausted, but I designed my research in a way I knew would work

(13)

Coercion and vulnerability

Of course we need to always be mindful of the perceived coercion and vulnerability for those who are involved in research taking part in research (15). It is imperative that participants enter into research of their own free will with the correct information given to them. It is thought, by some, that some may want to take part to have an influence on their case. However, this has been shown not to be the case if research is carried out ethically and to protocol (4) and research tells that in well-conducted research projects participants in the criminal justice system are keen to take part in research (4). Participants can be more difficult to follow-up because of chaotic lifestyles but it can be done (2, 40). This is important when devising projects and submitting ethical approvals but most importantly when explaining the study to the participants.

Ethical approval

All research which include participants where you are using their data need ethical approvals (41). It is important to note that ethical approvals take time and there are things to consider, as Matfin, 2011, cited in Ferguson 2022 states:

> If the proposed research findings would represent no intrinsic value to the Service, the research is unlikely to be sanctioned
>
> *(13, 42)*

Ethical approval for research in the criminal justice system is difficult primarily because of the correctly perceived coercion and vulnerability of the participants (43). However, Institutional Review Boards and other protective human subject mechanisms are necessary to maintain that vulnerable populations get the protection they require from taking part in research. Ethical approval will need to be sought from three sources: The University itself in the first instance, then by Her Majesty's Prison and Probation Services (HMPPS), either by Online Integrated Research Approval System (IRAS) or the excel application depending on the subject of the research, and the amount of prisons access is required to. An important point to note for ethical approval in a prison is that co-production is essential from day one. The first step, even prior to submitting ethical approval documents, is getting the Governor on board with the research. However, these processes are necessary to ensure that all work is undertaken ethically and legally, but it is important to be upfront with partners about the potential time implications of these processes at the start of the project before any time lines are agreed (29).

It has often been stated that practitioners and policymakers see translational research or knowledge exchange is one directional with the academics leading the work and doing the work for policymakers and practitioners (16). However, results from academic work can often take as long as 17 years to get things into practice (44) which often means the service has been closed and policy has moved on.

One of the major barriers to engaging academics in co-production work within certain policy and practitioner settings is the constraint put on the type of experiment that can be conducted. Although it is done, it would be unusual to be able to carry out a randomised controlled trial in a local authority setting, for example (16). Due to the hierarchy of evidence and the academic drive to publish in high impact journals, these settings may initially seem less attractive to academics (10, 12). However, through engaging in such co-production projects, academics will gain access to new types of data and study subjects and be able to get their research into practice at a much quicker pace (10).

Co-production gives us the chance to look at different kinds of science with readily available data and means we can do research quickly to fit within funding streams. The more recent focus on the need for research funders to look at 'natural experiments' is promising but underutilised (45).

Implementation science

It has been shown that a lack of research skills and the disparity in the terminologies used by academics and practitioners and policymakers could contribute to the 'research evidence-implementation' gap (46). Implementation science was born as a result of recognising the importance of this gap that exists between research and practice (47, 48). This gap has expedited the use of multitudinous theoretical constructs, aiming to enhance the implementation process, identify the barriers and facilitators and acting as valuable tools in evaluating implementation (49). Implementation science is commonly defined as the study of methods and strategies to promote the uptake of interventions that have proven effective into routine practice, with the aim of improving population health. Implementation science therefore examines what works, for whom and under what circumstances, and how interventions can be adapted and scaled up in ways that are accessible and equitable (50). We are now at an optimal time to use implementation science to enable evidence to be gotten into practice in a quicker way (47).

Co-production Is Tricky!

Co-production projects can be tricky (4, 15, 51); as with any industry, stakeholders working together face a number of challenges. For practitioners and policymakers, they need results fast and they need to be cost-effective and be applicable to an ever-changing policy climate and with time and budgetary constraints as well as taking into account commissioning cycles (15, 18, 29). We recommend, where possible, that honorary contracts at both institutions are helpful, so that each has access to systems and the ability to get into the building without buzzing people every time they come in (16). It has been shown that it can be helpful for practitioners and policymakers to have space within the university useful in terms of building networks, and providing protected time for space writing and access to supporting scientific publications. For the academics it has provided a critical opportunity to be immersed within policy/practice culture within the partner organisations (15, 26, 29).

One pressure point for working in co-production is the conflict between timescales, robustness and speed. Often policy and practice projects have tight deadlines to meet, which are linked to commissioning timescales and national policy demands (29). This need-for-speed can be at odds with traditional academic methods, which whilst thorough can often be long and drawn-out (29, 52). Therefore, careful negotiation may be required up-front to be open and honest around how long different phases of the research may take, and when milestones can feasibly be achieved, and deliverables provided (29). Whilst ideally a co-production project would involve an equal partnership, when time pressures arise, the academic partner is often required to take on the bulk of the work to ensure that projects remain on track (4, 29). Additionally, there is perhaps an assumption that commissioning decisions are linear. These decisions are subject to strict funding regimes, are bound in political tensions (national and local), follow a strict timeline and are led by one individual whose focus is just on that commission (16).

It is important for academics to be clear at the beginning that they are neutral and they may not get the results the practitioners and/or police makers want but they will be evidence based (29). However, in practice, these challenges are overcome through a shared focus on improving population health, and effective communication with all relevant stakeholders to ensure all expectations are managed from the projects inception (15, 29).

Sullivan and O'Neil argue that academics working with practitioners and policymakers also provide access to an institutional 'brand', which could mean that participants are more trusting and willing to engage with evaluations which is helpful to academics (16). In their book chapter, they point to important considerations from policymakers' and practitioners' view for co-producing research (16).

1. The organisation must be committed and the work the practitioners will be working on embedded into their work plans.
2. Timelines must be agreed and must take into account gaining ethical approvals.
3. The practitioner and organisation should not over commit. Agreement must be made of what is practicable to be done.
4. Find the right academic(s) to work with. This process is not for all academics. The passion to bring academic skills into the frontline work of public health and the opportunity to publish small-scale evaluations to add to the richness and diversity of the evidence base requires a true belief in translational research.

Sharing co-production evaluation learning and publication

One of the key aspirations of co-production for the authors has always been to achieve publications with peer-reviewed journals. The opportunity for the staff to develop the skills and competence to undertake quality-assured evaluations and subsequently participate in the development of a peer-reviewed journal article is not something often available at practitioner level. The authors of this book have aspired to do this and currently have published many articles with co-production partners including practitioners and policymakers in public health and or the criminal justice system (2–8, 12, 26, 53–65). We have also co-presented at conference such as the Public Health England and international conferences and university seminars.

We would encourage all academics to work in co-production where possible and promise you will learn so much from doing it. It is not for everyone but everyone should give it a go.

Chapter summary

This chapter has shown one way of working with practitioners and policymakers that the authors have used. Using co-production ways of working can be tricky and is not for all academics, or indeed every practitioner or policymaker; however, when it used well it can be transforming for making population change.

This book has shown that research in the criminal justice system is difficult; however, by looking at the link between alcohol, crime and public health and using a co-production methodology of working, for the right policymaker/practitioner and academics, you really can make a difference to peoples' lives.

References

1. Van Der Graaf P, Francis O, Doe E, Barrett E, O'Rorke M, Docherty G. Structural approaches to knowledge exchange: Comparing practices across five centres of excellence in public health. Journal of Public Health. 2018;40(1):i31–8.
2. Newbury-Birch D, Coulton S, Bland M, Cassidy P, Dale V, Deluca P, et al. Alcohol screening and brief interventions for offenders in the probation setting (SIPS Trial): A pragmatic multicentre cluster randomised controlled trial. Alcohol and Alcoholism. 2014;49(5):540–8.
3. Sherman L, Strang H, Barnes G, Bennett S, Angel C, Newbury-Birch D, et al. Restorative justice: The evidence. London: Smith Institute; 2007.
4. Sherman L, Strang H, Barnes G, Woods D, Bennett S, Inkpen N, et al. Twelve experiments in restorative justice: The jerry lee program of randomized trials of restorative justice conferences. Journal of Experimental Criminology. 2015;11:501–40.
5. Holloway A, Ferguson J, Parker R, Sheik A, Guthrie V, Newbury-Birch D. Alcohol brief interventions for male remand prisoners: A mixed-methods feasibility and acceptability study. Lancet. 2019;394:S53.

6. Holloway A, Guthrie V, Waller G, Smith J, Boyd J, Mercado S, et al. A two-arm parallel-group individually randomised prison pilot study of a male remand alcohol intervention for self-efficacy enhancement: The APPRAISE study protocol. BMJ Open. 2021;11(4):e040636.

7. Holloway A, Landale S, Ferguson J, Newbury-Birch D, Parker R, Smith P, et al. Alcohol Brief Interventions for male remand prisoners: Protocol for a complex intervention framework development and feasibility study. BMJ Open. 2017;7(4).

8. Addison M, McGovern R, Angus C, Becker F, Brennan A, Brown H, et al. Alcohol screening and brief intervention in police custody suites: Pilot Cluster Randomised Controlled Trial (AcCePT). Alcohol and Alcoholism. 2018;53(5):548–59.

9. Armstrong RP, Pettman TL , Waters E. Shifting sands – From description to solutions. Public Health. 2014;128(6):525–32.

10. Newbury-Birch D, McGeechan G, Holloway A. Climbing down the steps from the ivory tower: How UK academics and criminal justice practitioners need to work together on alcohol studies. International Journal of Prisoner Health. 2016;12(3):129–34.

11. Newbury-Birch D, McGovern R, Birch J, O'Neill G, Kaner H, Sondhi A, et al. A rapid systematic review of what we know about alcohol use disorders and brief interventions in the criminal justice system. International Journal of Prisoner Health. 2016;12(1):57–70.

12. Sondhi A, Birch J, Lynch K, Holloway A, Newbury-Birch D. Exploration of delivering brief interventions in a prison setting: A qualitative study in one English region. Drugs Education, Prevention and Policy. 2016; 23(5):382–7, doi:10.1080/09687637.2016.1183588

13. Ferguson J. Examining the feasibility of carrying out alcohol screening and brief interventions for women in an open prison setting. Middlesbrough: Teesside University; 2022.

14. Lancet Gastroenterology Hepatology. Public health funding in England: Death by a thousand cuts. Lancet Gastroenterology & Hepatology. 2021;6(12):971.

15. Newbury-Birch D, McGeechan G, Holloway A. Climbing down the steps from the ivory tower: How UK academics and practitioners need to work together on alcohol studies (Editorial). International Journal of Prisoner Health. 2016;12(3):129–34.

16. Sullivan C, O'Neil G. Chapter 1: Why should we co-produce research? In: Newbury-Birch D, Allan K (eds.) Co-creating and co-producing research evidence: A guide for practitioners and academics in health, social care and education settings. London: Routledge; 2019. pp. 1–8.

17. Kneale J, French S. Mapping alcohol: Health, policy and the geographies of problem drinking in Britain. Drugs: Education, Prevention, and Policy. 2008;15(3):233–49.

18. Cheetham M, Redgate S, van der Graaf P, Humble C, Hunter D, Adamson A. 'What I really want is academics who want to partner and who care about the outcome': Findings from a mixed-methods study of evidence use in local government in England. Evidence & Policy. 2022;19(1):74–94. Retrieved Feb 8, 2023, from https://bristoluniversitypressdigital.com/view/journals/evp/19/1/article-p74.xml

19. Sherman L. Evidence-based policing. Washington: Policing Institute; 1998. Available from: www.policefoundation.org

20. Shepherd J. How to achieve more effective services: The evidence eco-system. Cardiff: Cardiff University; 2014.

21. Pettman T, Armstrong R, Doyle J, Burford B, Anderson L, Hilgrove T, et al. Strengthening evaluation to capture the breadth of public health practice: Ideal vs real. Journal of Public Health. 2012;37(2):151–55.

22. Wehrens R. Beyond two communities – from research utilization and knowledge translation to coproduction? Public Health. 2014;128(6):545–51.
23. Graham ID, Tetroe J. How to translate health research knowledge into effective healthcare action. Healthcare Q. 2007;10:20–2.
24. Verschuere B, Brandsen T, Pestoff V. Co-production: The state of the art in research and the future agenda. Voluntas: International Journal of Voluntary and Nonprofit Organizations. 2012;23(4):1083–101.
25. Realpe A, Wallace L. What is co-production? London: The Health Foundation; 2010.
26. Newbury-Birch D, Allan K. Co-creating and co-producing research evidence: A guide for practitioners and academics in health, social care and education settings. London: Routledge; 2020.
27. Sherman LW, Strang H, Barnes G, Woods DJ, Bennett S, Inkpen N, et al. Twelve experiments in restorative justice: The Jerry Lee program of randomized trials of restorative justice conferences. Journal of Experimental Criminology. 2015;11(4):501–40.
28. Coulton S, Nizalova O, Pellatt-Higgins T, Stevens A, Hendrie N, Marchand C, et al. Pragmatic randomized controlled trial to evaluate the effectiveness and cost-effectiveness of a multi-component intervention to reduce substance use and risk-taking behaviour in adolescents involved in the criminal justice system: A trial protocol (RISKIT-CJS). BMC Public Health. 2017;17:246. https://doi.org/10.1186/s12889-017-4170-6
29. McGeechan G, Ells L, Giles E. Chapter 2: Co-production: The academic perspective. In: Newbury-Birch D, Allan K (eds.) Co-creating and co-producing research evidence: A guide for practitioners and academics in health, social care and education settings. London: Routledge; 2019. pp. 9–20.
30. Graham I, Logan J, Harrison M, Straus S, Tetroe J, Caswell W. Lost in knowledge translation: Time for a map? Journal of Continuing Education in the Health Professions. 2006;26:13–24.
31. McIntyre A. Participatory action research, Vol. 52. California: Sage; 2007.
32. Grimshaw JM, Eccles MP, Lavis JN, Hill SJ, Squires JE. Knowledge translation of research findings. Implementation Science. 2012;7:50.
33. Bloedon R, Stokes D. Making university/industry collaborative research succeed. Research-Technology Management. 1994;37(2):44–8.
34. Tetroe J. Knowledge translation at the Canadian Institutes of Health Research: A primer. Focus Tech Brief. 2007:1–8.
35. Morris Z, Wooding S, Grant J. The answer is 17 years, what is the question: Understanding time lags in translational research. Journal of the Royal Society of Medicine. 2011;104(12):510–20.
36. Guston D. Stabilizing the boundary between US politics and science: The role of the Office of Technology Transfer as a boundary organization. Social Studies of Science. 1999;29(1):87–111.
37. Miller C. Hybrid management: Boundary organizations, science policy, and environmental governance in the climate regime. Science, Technology & Human Values Autumn. 2001;26:478–500.
38. Goffman E. The presentation of self in everyday life. London: Harmondsworth; 1990.
39. Wenger E, McDermott R, Snyder W. Cultivating communities of practice: A guide to managing knowledge. Boston: Harvard Business Press; 2002.
40. Newbury-Birch D, McGovern R, Birch J, Kaner H, O'Neill G. Alcohol Screening and Brief Intervention (ASBI) in the Prison System Factsheet. 2014. http://therapeutic-solutions.org.uk/assets/static/proposals/Prison_Factsheet.pdf

41. Smajdor A, Sydes MR, Gelling L, Wilkinson M. Applying for ethical approval for research in the United Kingdom. BMJ. 2009;339:b4013.
42. Matfin C. Doing research in a prison setting. In: Jupp V, Davies P, Francis P (eds.) Doing Criminological Research. London: Sage Publications; 2011. pp. 215–33.
43. Jones J. Ethical considerations in criminal justice research: Informed consent and confidentiality. Inquiries Journal/Student Pulse. 2012;4(8):1–2.
44. Morris Z, Wooding S, Grant J. The answer is 17 years, what is the question: Understanding time lags in translational research. Journal of the Royal Society of Medicine. 2011;104(12):510–20.
45. Petticrew M, Cummins S, Ferrell C, Findlay A, Higgins C, Hoy C, et al. Natural experiments: An underused tool for public health? Public Health. 2005;119(9):751–7.
46. Friese B, Bogenshneider K. The voice of experience: How social scientists communicate family research to policymakers. Family Relationships. 2009;58(2):229–43.
47. Waller G, Finch T, Giles E, Newbury-Birch D. Implementation of tobacco and substance use interventions within a secondary school setting: A systematic review. Implementation Science. 2017;12(1):130–48.
48. Glasgow RE, Lichtenstein E, Marcus AC. Why don't we see more translation of health promotion research to practice? Rethinking the efficacy-to-effectiveness transition. AJPH. 2003;93(8):1261–7.
49. May C, Finch T. Implementation, embedding, and integration: An outline of normalization process theory. Sociology. 2009;43(3):535–54.
50. Michie S, Fixsen D, Grimshaw JM, Eccles MP. Specifying and reporting complex behaviour change interventions: The need for a scientific method. Implementation Science. 2009;4(1):40.
51. Byng R, Kirkpatrick T, Lennox C, Warren FC, Anderson R, Brand SL ... Shaw J. Evaluation of a complex intervention for prisoners with common mental health problems, near to and after release: The Engager randomised controlled trial. The British Journal of Psychiatry. 2023;222(1):18–26. doi:10.1192/bjp.2022.93
52. Martin S. Co-production of social research: Strategies for engaged scholarship. Public Money & Management. 2010;30(4):211–8. doi: 10.1080/09540962.2010.492180
53. McGeechan GJ, Wilkinson KG, Martin N, Wilson L, O'Neill G, Newbury-Birch D. A mixed-method outcome evaluation of a specialist Alcohol Hospital Liaison Team. Perspectives in Public Health. 2016;136(6):361–7.
54. McGeechan GJ, Woodall D, Anderson L, Wilson L, O'Neill G, Newbury-Birch D. A coproduction community based approach to reducing smoking prevalence in a local community setting. Journal of Environmental and Public Health. 2016;2016(1):5386534. doi: 10.1155/2016/5386534
55. McGeechan G, Richardson C, Weir K, Wilson L, O'Neill G, Newbury-Birch D. Evaluation of a pilot police-led suicide early alert surveillance strategy in the UK. Injury Prevention. 2018;24:267–71.
56. McParlin C, O'Donnell A, Robson S, Beyer F, Molony E, Bryant A, et al. Treatments for hyperemesis gravidarum and nausea and vomiting in pregnancy: A systematic review. JAMA. 2016;316(13):1392–401.
57. Camilleri N, Newbury-Birch D, McArdle P, Stocken DD, Thick T, Le Couteur A. Innovations in practice: A case control and follow-up study of 'hard to reach' young people who suffered from multiple complex mental disorders. Child and Adolescent Mental Health. 2017;22(1):49–57.
58. Al-Jefri K, Newbury-Birch D, Muirhead CR, Gilvarry E, Araújo-Soares V, Reynolds NJ, et al. High prevalence of alcohol use disorders in patients with inflammatory skin diseases. British Journal of Dermatology. 2017;177(3):837–44.

59. Glencorse M, Wilson G, Newbury-Birch D. Paramedic perceptions and attitudes to working with patients with alcohol-related injury and illness. Journal of Paramedic Practice. 2014;6(6):310–8.

60. Sullivan C, Martin N, White C, Newbury-Birch D. Assessing the delivery of alcohol screening and brief intervention in sexual health clinics in the north east of England. BMC Public Health. 2017;17(1):884. https://doi.org/10.1186/s12889-017-4878-3

61. Wilson G, Wray C, Mcgovern R, Newbury-Birch D, McColl E, Crosland A, et al. Intervention to reduce excessive alcohol consumption and improve comorbid outcomes in hypertensive or depressed primary care patients: Two parallel cluster randomised feasibility trials. BMC Trials. 2014;15(235):1–15.

62. Martin N, Buykx P, Shevills C, Sullivan C, Clark L, Newbury-Birch D. Population level effects of a mass media alcohol and breast cancer campaign: A cross-sectional pre-intervention and post-intervention evaluation. Alcohol and Alcoholism. 2018;53(1):31–8.

63. Hayden C, Moat C, Newbury-Birch D. An analysis of ambulance data to ascertain the prevalence and demographics of individuals who have died by suicide. Emergency Nurse. 2020;29(1):35–40.

64. Parkinson K, Newbury-Birch D, Phillipson A, Hindmarch P, Kaner E, Stamp E, et al. Prevalence of alcohol related attendance at an inner city emergency department and its impact: A dual prospective and retrospective cohort study. 2016;33(3):187–93.

65. Bogowicz P, Ferguson J, Gilvarry E, Kamali F, Kaner E, Newbury-Birch D. Alcohol and other substance use among medical and law students at a UK university: A cross sectional questionnaire survey. Postgraduate Medical Journal. 2018;94:131–6.

INDEX

Note: Page numbers in *italics* indicate figures, **bold** indicate tables in the text.

Printed in the United States
by Baker & Taylor Publisher Services

Printed in the United States
by Baker & Taylor Publisher Services